FINDYOUR DIFFERENCE

FIND YOUR DIFFERENCE

CHALLENGING CONFORMITY
IN BUSINESS
AND IN LIFE

AUSTIN McGHIE

SILICON
VALLEY
PRESS

Published by Silicon Valley Press, Carmel, CA
Siliconvalleypress.net

Cover design: Philippe Becker

ISBN (hardcover): 978-1-7358731-3-8
ISBN (ebook): 978-1-7358731-4-5
LCCN: 2021910763

First edition

"Why fit in when you were born to stand out?"

—Dr. Seuss

CONTENTS

Foreword ix

Preface xi

Chapter 0 3

PART I: THE CASE FOR DIFFERENCE

Chapter 1: Opening the Door to Difference 9

Chapter 2: The Science of Difference 34

Chapter 3: What's Really Going on Here? 49

PART II: DIFFERENCE DAMPENERS

Chapter 4: Our Parents and Our Institutions 83

Chapter 5: Our Companies 92

Chapter 6: Our Selves 107

PART III: THE REAL-WORLD CREATION OF DIFFERENCE

Chapter 7: Finding Difference in Three Business Scenarios . . . 121

Chapter 8: How to Create Differentiated Advantage: A Process . 135

Chapter 9: Ten Things to Consider as You Pursue Difference . . 164

Chapter 10: Getting People on Board 195

Chapter 11: Difference in Execution 202

Chapter 12: Parting Thoughts 211

Acknowledgments 219

About the Author 221

FOREWORD

Austin McGhie's belief that true difference is the engine that propels great brands is absolute. In fact, I sometimes wonder if it's a conviction so deeply held that it's made its way into his DNA.

As business partners, Austin and I debate the "difference quotient" of our recommendations on an almost daily basis. However, we rarely lose sight of the fact that the forces of orthodoxy and inertia are far stronger than most people's desire to uproot the status quo.

While there is lots of rhetoric and chatter in business about reinvention and disruption, there is enormous reticence to actually walk the talk. As Austin has often quoted, "The only one who likes change is a wet baby."

One interesting evolution has been seeing Austin espouse the virtues of difference beyond business—in life at large. Of COVID's many revelations, surely the most obvious one is that business as usual is the ultimate air castle.

A future-ready human race doesn't need more of the same. As a society, we need to embrace difference to face and ace the challenges of the twenty-first century.

The trick in all of this is not to seek difference for its own sake— there are so many examples of vapid, lame, desperate difference out there—but that's for another book.

The real opportunity for business and individuals alike is to find what makes you different in a way that makes you better—and then to use your difference to build a better world.

Like the indispensable *Positioning: The Battle for Your Mind* by Al Ries and Jack Trout, or the masterful *Zag* by Marty Neumeier, Austin's *Find Your Difference* is both timely and evergreen. It really is a must read.

Alpa Pandya

PREFACE

We love difference, but we hate to be different.

We celebrate and follow those who are truly unique, yet we shy away from doing something completely different ourselves.

We speak longingly of the path not taken, yet we never walk it.

While most marketers understand that brands and businesses reach the upper echelons of success only when they offer something truly unique, these same people fail to take the risk of doing something completely different.

Why?

As a marketing strategist, I have come up against this question countless times in my forty-year career. In these pages, I attempt to answer it.

This is a book for working marketers. If you want to sell anything—a product, a service, a company, an idea, a place, or a personality—you are a marketer. Because business runs on selling products and services to people, business runs on marketing. Sooner or later, regardless of profession, we all need to sell our ideas to others, so we're all working marketers of some kind. Of course, this would suggest that every single human being should read this book.

Isn't marketing great?

As a marketer, no matter the size or shape of your endeavor or what you are selling, if you want to succeed, you need to find and then market your difference. Strategically and tactically, difference is the engine room of great marketing.

If you are trying to build your own brand or business, difference is the key. Find the one thing that differentiates you in the most compelling way possible, and you will win. Failure to do different leads to marketing mediocrity. Without difference, you will work much harder than those who succeed, with much less to show for your effort.

If difference is central to marketing, why do we see it so rarely?

Herein lies the challenge: Difference is the most important yet most elusive construct in marketing. The gap between understanding the importance of difference and actually creating it is massive. It's a chasm that only the best and bravest marketers cross.

I want to show you how.

This book is part exploration and part exhortation—part *Why does this chasm exist?* and part *How can you cross it?* Because if you want to succeed, you've got to get to the other side. You've got to take the leap.

The difficulty with difference is found not in understanding but in action. I can offer understanding, but the action will be up to you.

Ready? Here is the itinerary for your trip across that chasm:

Part I: The Case for Difference

Successful brands and businesses are built on difference. Through a combination of subjective opinion, war stories, and inarguable data, I'll prove this thesis once and for all, then we can move on.

Part II: Difference Dampeners

Doing something completely different makes the vast majority of us uncomfortable. Really uncomfortable. We'll explore the underpinnings of this discomfort and see how we might get out of our own way.

Part III: The Real-World Creation of Difference

Now that you're determined to do different, this practical guide will show you how to find and create difference in business, strategically and tactically.

Along the way, I hope this exploration of difference will challenge you, inspire you, and—most importantly—help you.

As I've written this book, exploring difference has taken me to some unexpected places. For example, I've come to realize how important diversity is in the day-to-day creation of difference— diversity of every possible kind. Homogeneity and weakly held beliefs are enemies of difference. So I'll make an impassioned case for diversity, not as corporate obligation but as an important source of competitive advantage.

Further, I've come to realize that any thorough discussion of difference must acknowledge its shadow. In business, we succeed by being unique in a way that is better than our competitors. In life, however, applying relative value to difference—the notion that two things can't just be different, but one must be "better"—causes extraordinary damage. How might the world change if we celebrated difference in equal measure?

Fundamentally, this is a business book, yet I hope it is more. I hope you learn something new, but, more importantly, I hope you think something new.

Let's get going.

"The person who follows the crowd will usually go no further than the crowd. The person who walks alone is likely to find himself in places no one has ever seen before."
—Albert Einstein

CHAPTER 0

LET'S START WITH SOME FINAL THOUGHTS

"One person can make a difference, and everyone should try."
—John F. Kennedy

Once upon a time, in a city far, far away, I was an overconfident, highly ambitious little assistant brand manager, fresh out of MBA school. The son of a leading clinical psychologist, I had fallen in love with marketing as some sort of exercise in art meets business meets psychology. I couldn't wait to get started in my new life—with my new suit and my shiny new credit card.

Never in school did I so much as catch a mention of "difference." For several years as a packaged goods brand marketer, theoretically at the top of my trade, no one I worked for stressed the importance of difference. We "built brands," "drove volume," and "gained market share"—but difference was MIA. Come to think of it, we didn't even measure it. We tracked so many key variables it'd make your head spin, but not that one.

Did I waste my twenties? I certainly missed an opportunity to make a lot of money tracking difference for others, but who would have believed the fresh-faced guy in the new suit?

I didn't find religion until I heard of this thing called Brand Asset Valuator, created by my employer at the time, Young & Rubicam. From that day on, I became increasingly fascinated by the power of difference. Power that has been proven, again and again, but that most of us shy away from, as we'll discuss at some length.

Difference is highly attractive conceptually but scares most of us in practice. We might think different but balk at actually doing different. We seem to acknowledge and even appreciate how we differ inside our own heads, yet we conform when dealing with the world around us. Why?

I'm writing this introduction having already finished my book and sent it to friends in the hope they'll enjoy it and write something nice I can use on the back cover. One consistent piece of feedback really stood out to me and spurred me to add a chapter 0. The thought runs something along the lines of *You should have done more with this idea of DQ—it's catchy.*

The irony is that DQ, or Difference Quotient, was one of the last thoughts I had as I wrote my little heart out. I wish I'd thought of it much earlier, as a catchy way to show what I think we're all missing. As you read the book, you'll run across DQ several times—the general idea being that we highly value IQ and EQ (intelligence and emotional quotients), yet approach DQ with great caution. I actually toyed with the idea of using DQ as the title, but right or wrong, I ultimately found using DQ as a title to be a bit too clichéd.

Personally, I think my own DQ was always pretty high. I was a geek long before Silicon Valley made the word popular. But I have to admit that I, like so many others, did not resist the urge to fit in. In many ways, I wasted the high DQ of my youth and didn't get religion until my more "mature" years. Good at sports, I approached my business career the same way, competing within the lines and trying to prove I was better. Better, not different, was the name of the game.

But, as I hope you will agree after reading my book, the right kind of difference is the best possible kind of better. As many brave entrepreneurs (all, I would argue, with a high DQ) have shown us, playing outside the lines and inventing your own set of rules is the best possible way to go. This assumes, of course, that you have some desire to be fabulously successful and wealthy. If this simply isn't the case, just stay inside the lines and stick to the rules.

Conform.

While this is a business book, it's also an open invitation to challenge conformity. An invitation to embrace whatever makes you unique. Embrace whatever makes others unique. An invitation for all of us to stop searching for similarity in those around us and instead look for—and celebrate—difference.

Let's face it, the world's differences are way more interesting than the world's similarities!

PART I

THE CASE FOR DIFFERENCE

"Every man and woman is born into the world to do something unique and something distinctive, and if he or she does not do it, it will never be done."

—Benjamin E. Mays

CHAPTER 1

OPENING THE DOOR TO DIFFERENCE

"The moment you doubt you can fly, you cease forever to be able to do it."

—J. M. Barrie, *Peter Pan*

Ideally, we would be sitting in a conference room or lecture hall right now, engaging in a dynamic exchange of exciting, sometimes opposing perspectives on difference. Actually, better still, we'd be sitting at the pub having a pint. Instead of walking into that pub, you've walked into this book, so you're stuck with a decidedly one-way conversation. After four decades of pushing for difference, I think I've managed to learn a few things (often the hard way), so I hope you'll find value in the monologue.

Let's get warmed up with an overview of the key ideas and opinions you'll encounter in this book.

GREAT BUSINESSES AND BRANDS ARE
BUILT ON STRENGTH OF DIFFERENCE.

This is not only one of the most important ideas in marketing, but also plain old common sense: businesses sell things to humans; humans pay attention to things that stand out. Back when we were scantily clad bipeds roaming the open plains, noticing difference was a critically important survival mechanism. Today, though our lives are significantly less dependent upon it, we still can't help but attend to uniqueness. As intellectually and emotionally curious beings, we are drawn to it like moths to a flame. If for no other reason, people who are selling ideas should embrace difference simply because it gets noticed.

The capacity to stand out amid marketplace noise has never been more important to the working marketer. As anyone who browses Amazon, navigates Netflix, or walks through a grocery aisle knows, the market has become incredibly cluttered. The resulting tyranny of choice can prove daunting to potential buyers trying to make the purchase that will meet their needs. Difference can only become even more important in the future. Yes, our "attention filters" will become increasingly sophisticated, but as long as people keep creating more choices, the importance of standing out will continue to grow.

When it's foggy, you need a really bright light to get noticed. When it's cluttered, you need to be highly differentiated to stand out.

The importance of difference is one of the few demonstrably true and scientifically supported facts in the often vague, but usually well-articulated, world of marketing. Difference is a leading indicator. Enhance it, and good things will happen—to market share, revenue, profitability, and shareholder value. Let it drop, and the opposite is true. (We'll get to the data that proves this later; for now, just trust me.)

Of course, it doesn't take much to stand out. Any idiot can sashay down the street naked, playing "Come Follow the Band" on bagpipes while banging cymbals between their knees. But few people will take up the invitation. Because that's dumb difference—rebel without a cause.

Smart difference is meaningful—rebel *with* a cause. Difference must be compelling to your audience, a path to competitive advantage—the hard part that makes everything easier. Without it, you can work your marketing butt off, but the outcome is fated to be mediocre. Middle of the road. Vanilla.

Importantly, I'm talking about difference in an absolute sense: not simply against a few key competitors, but against all the other brands, businesses, and ideas our audience has in their heads. In the absolute, we have to be as unique as possible. We have to stand out.

BUSINESS IS MARKETING. MARKETING IS POSITIONING. POSITIONING IS DIFFERENCE.

Peter Drucker once said that a business has only two basic functions: marketing and innovation. In my mind, both of these functions rely heavily on difference. Drucker also stated that the sole purpose of business is to create a customer. Creating a customer has become more difficult over time, as an ever-increasing number of products, services, and ideas are in hot pursuit of that same customer, doing everything possible to attract their attention.

If you want to create a customer, you need to know how to position the thing you are selling to them. It really is that simple. Imagine yourself at a dinner table with friends, trying to sell them on an idea. You know these people well, and almost without conscious thought, you are weighing different ways to present that idea, looking for the one with the highest chance of success. You are engaging in the dark art of positioning.

If you're a working marketer and you can read only one book (in addition to mine, of course), read *Positioning*, by Al Ries and Jack Trout. This book sold me on marketing when I was a young assistant brand manager, and its premise remains important. (Yes, it may be a bit dated at this point, but read it anyway.)

In the simplest terms possible, here's the premise: your position is the one unique, true idea you will seek to become famous for. Note: It's one idea—not two ideas disguised as one. It's unique—as proprietary as possible. It's true—faithful to your product or service.

Imagine a position as an idea that acts as your front door. In this metaphor, your business is a house comprised of meticulously designed rooms filled with complex, beautiful stuff. You worked really hard to design this interior. You believe—no, you know—it's the best house in the neighborhood. You're convinced people would love it, if you could just get them to step through the front door. Too many marketers want to tell us all about their house and the wonderful features inside, but real people simply don't have the time or the attention span for this kind of conversation.

Here's the challenge: there are a lot of houses out there, and it's your job to attract people to your house and invite them in. In the middle of a colorful, creative, high-density neighborhood, your front door has to stand out from all the others. How do you make your front door—your position—irresistibly attractive to your intended audience? How do you pull focus from all those other doors onto yours? What is the one truly unique idea that will invite your audience in so they can see your home's beautifully designed interior?

If you want to sell something, you need to know how to position it. Many of us started practicing this skill early in life (poorly, in my case), when we blamed a younger sibling for a mess we created. Salespeople are the masters of on-the-fly positioning, changing their approach as a pitch evolves in real time. Politicians, too, are constantly positioning their ideas to gain the support of their constituents.

As a poignant example, take 9/11. We could have positioned that attack as a horrific crime, perpetrated by a criminal gang. In the weeks that followed that terrible event, the world was ready to help us find and prosecute these criminals. We could have—and I believe should have—organized the world's biggest manhunt for the criminals who committed this mass murder.

But that's not the position our government chose.

Instead they positioned our response as a "war on terrorism." Wars are fought by the military. Wars are prosecuted by soldiers, not the police. In a war, you call the criminals "enemy combatants." Once everyone embraced this superficially inspiring "war on terrorism," it was only a matter of time before we invaded nations. We rebranded murderers as combatants, to better fit the construct of war, thereby giving them credibility they did not deserve.

You can guess how I would have positioned our response, but my point is this: a subtle use of language established a clear position. It described a choice. It drove our country down one path instead of another.

In politics they are more likely to refer to this as "framing," but it is positioning. As a liberal, I can only bemoan the fact that the Republican Party seems to be much better than the Democratic Party at positioning. While the right seems to quickly settle on a short, catchy phrase that they use with great consistency to position a single idea, the left spends its time debating the complexity of that idea. In the world of positioning, "Let's simplify this" will always beat "It's more complicated than that."

Back to business.

Marketers need to determine one clear, unique, and consistent position—an idea that can stand the test of time and competitive pressure. As a marketer, if you consistently position something over

time, you can build what we call a "brand." As I discussed in my
first book, *Brand Is a Four Letter Word*, the B-word may be the most
abused and misunderstood word in business. *Brand* is a noun, not a
verb. It's the prize, and it has real value, but it's never a verb (unless
you have cattle). You can name, design, and market something, but
you can't brand it; you position it. And if you position it effectively
and consistently, over time you will build a brand. Positioning is
the verb. Positioning is the work.

Marketing is positioning. Positioning is difference. At times I
will talk about positioning and difference as if they are one idea, as
positioning success inherently relies on the ability to find your difference. For clarity, I will also explore them as two separate, though
mutually supportive, ideas.

Whatever we're selling, we must position it in a way that is
focused, unique, compelling, and culturally noisy. Four ideas in one
short sentence. We'll explore them in more detail later, but for now
know this: Any position must have focus and difference—focus to
keep you on a straight and narrow path, and difference to ensure
you are not dutifully walking the same path as others. Many bad
ideas are unique, so your position also must contain competitive
advantage and be compelling to your audience. At some point,
that position must drive marketing expression, so your difference
should contain dramatic tension as well, meaning it should be as
culturally noisy as possible. We'll continue this part of the conversation as we proceed.

DIFFERENCE IS CREATED, NOT CONSTRUCTED.

When I give my "difference sermon" in speeches and meetings,
almost everyone in the room nods knowingly. I'm not sure anyone has ever argued against difference at a conceptual level. Still,
I worry that this apparent agreement is superficial, so I've learned

to push the point as far as my audience will allow. I attempt to convey that the difference I'm talking about will feel, well, different. Foreign. Even radical. I warn that true difference makes most of us feel uncomfortable.

Let me pick on consumer packaged goods (CPG) marketing for a minute. Historically the continuing education hub for professional marketing, CPG companies, I would argue, are still home to the most sophisticated marketing available. However, for the purpose of difference creation, these companies are often too focused on their product features and benefits, consumer insights, target audience, and competitive advantages. CPG marketers are incredibly well informed and manage their brands very carefully along these dimensions.

At times, though, it's a lot of trees and no forest.

This approach isn't wrong; it's just not right enough. It's too incremental. It optimizes rather than creating something totally unique. Too often, it misses two very important and related marketing opportunities: difference and cultural meaning.

Done well, difference creates a very clear choice in the marketplace, and this is a challenging idea for many marketers: *If I'm different from everyone else, what if they're right and I'm wrong? When the choice is made clear, what if my audience doesn't pick me?* Difference is an absolute. As a more incremental practice, CPG marketing doesn't do well with absolutes. Further, as we'll discuss, true difference often involves a huge, intuitive leap. A leap of faith. CPG marketing—notoriously data driven and highly analytical—doesn't do well with faith.

At its best, difference defines a brand in a way that can influence, even lead, culture. Ideally you want a position so provocative and culturally meaningful that it sparks active discussion in noncommercial circles. To see an example, watch the YouTube video "Designed by Apple in California." It's safe to say that Apple understands culturally meaningful difference.

One of the dangers inherent to the rigorous art of CPG marketing is that the sheer amount of analysis and insight can force thinking into a small space, thereby missing much larger cultural opportunities. Again, these are sophisticated, highly analytical marketers. The analysis can ensure they won't get the answer wrong but can't ensure they'll get it right. We'll talk about this again later, but you can make a strong case for the idea that all this analysis simply gets you to the same conclusions that your competitors are equally busy reaching. Oops—where'd that difference go?

To be clear, in many ways, CPG marketing remains state-of-the-art, though the benefits of scale just ain't what they used to be, and these marketers face an increasingly tough marketplace.

Despite an incredibly cluttered long tail of craft and local competition, though, CPG marketing has also created several pretty inspiring difference stories, some of which we'll discuss later: Dove and Axe. Old Spice and Always. Miller Lite and Corona.

Ultimately, to attain real difference, we need to think with both sides of our brains, to learn how to graft the more absolute and culturally intuitive practice of difference creation onto the disciplined sophistication of CPG-style marketing.

Ultimately, difference is created, not constructed.

In business, analysis and proof will always speak louder than intuition and creativity—which is as it should be. But, as I've started to argue, if you arrive at a solution purely analytically, you must assume that others have arrived at exactly the same place. Do your homework better than the competition, but do it with the knowledge that true difference, almost by definition, will require a bold leap into uncharted territory.

BEWARE THE GRAY MIDDLE.

Moving from the world of CPG marketing to the world of the entrepreneur, allow me to hand the microphone to Sir Richard Branson, founder of the Virgin Group, an individualist and difference-maker if ever there was one:

> Name a role-model. Are they "normal"? Name somebody you love. Are they "normal"? I very much doubt it. Everybody should strive to be exceptional. The world is made up of extraordinary people. Don't waste your time trying to be normal. I've always been a square peg in a round hole, and I like it that way.

Branson has sustained some major failures, because that happens when you're swinging for the fences. Overall, he has led a spectacularly successful business life, and his personal life is every bit as unique. Like other entrepreneurs I'll talk about later, Branson sees the world through a radically different lens. His DQ (that's right, I'm coining a new term that will now spread like wildfire across the business landscape: "Difference Quotient") is extremely high. So high most of us would need oxygen and some serious anti-anxiety medication to breathe freely at Branson's elevation.

Many people understand the importance of difference on an intellectual level. A much smaller number, like Branson, have the attitude, nerve, and perseverance required to actually do different. These people come to difference naturally but, with some practice, the rest of us can most definitely close the gap.

If we have the science to prove the importance of difference (and as you will see, we do), why is it so hard to find in the wilds of business?

When I discuss marketing strategy with business executives, I like to present binary choices. For someone who knows every nuance of their business, being presented with a choice between black or white is challenging, and you can see that challenge play out as they are forced to choose. Some execs—those with higher DQ—understand the challenge immediately and choose quickly. With others, I need to qualify my request, prepare them with language like "I know this will seem extreme, but . . ."

I have a long history of creating a black-versus-white strategic scenario, only to see a business push for the gray that sits in between.

Like a black hole, the gray middle exerts an incredibly strong gravitational pull. The middle is comfortable. You can learn from all the other people inhabiting that space. If you choose the middle, you probably won't lose your job, at least this year, as long as you find ways to optimize your piece of the gray. Things happen more incrementally in the middle. When you opt for something gray, your neck is in rather than out. Most people don't second-guess the gray; it's not a place where things crash and burn. Instead they die a slow, slow death.

The gray middle is a failure-avoidance zone. The middle can never be proven wrong; it's just not sufficiently right.

And we're back to that nagging question: If the gray middle is not a place where people truly succeed, why do so many businesspeople heed its siren song? Why choose gray, when difference demands black or white? Yes, I realize it is much easier for me, as a consultant, to recommend difference than it is to do different. Business leaders often have a responsibility to thousands of people, and difference seems inherently risky to anyone in their position. But I will argue that the more dangerous choice is to take no risk at all.

FOCUS NARROW, CATCH WIDE.

Difference requires focus: a singular commitment to a unique idea. In fact, difference is pretty much impossible to achieve without focus. But focus makes people nervous: *If I'm too different, some people won't like me,* they think. *If I'm highly focused, I'll need to pass on opportunities I can see in my peripheral vision,* they fear.

They are operating under a false premise that goes something like this: The more people who like me, the more products and services I can provide, the more revenue I can generate, right?

So, so tragically wrong.

I get this way of thinking. I really do get it. It's like a misplaced version of stimulus > response. If you want a mass market (desired response), you need to take a position that appeals to everyone (assumed stimulus).

I propose that the opposite is true.

Later we'll talk about an idea my business partner, the brilliant Alpa Pandya, calls "target narrow, catch wide," which counters the belief that marketing to a mass audience is the only way to attract one. In short, the strongest brands we know operate as if they're designed for a very specific audience. The trick is that the rest of us find that specific audience highly aspirational. We see (or would like to see) at least a bit of those people in ourselves. We want to join that club, wear that badge.

More to come on this later.

BETTER IS NOT DIFFERENT.

To be really successful in business, you need to be competitive. Fiercely competitive. Competitive to a fault. Competitive in ways that might cause you to lose friends. In general, competitiveness is an asset in business, but a word of caution: harnessed in the wrong way, it can be the enemy of difference. Competitive myopia can also lead to some really bad decisions (remember New Coke?).

Once you pit a bunch of products and their marketers against one another, there's a real risk that they will become driven solely by the need to be better than each other, in as many ways as possible. Beer marketers were so busy trying to best the competition in the beer market, they missed the fact that young people were gravitating to spirits. Regardless, they continued to compete hard with each other, while a fourth category, led by hard lemonade and hard seltzer, started stealing away that young audience.

Don't get me wrong, competitiveness is really important. It's essential to success, but alone it's completely insufficient if you want to actually win.

The battle to be better, while important, must always work in support of the war to be unique.

Categories of industry, like people, develop habits. They lock into patterns. Marketers within a category often use similar language and source the same research. They tend to hire people with "category experience," a notion that has always intrigued me. If you believe that the path to success is difference, do you really want to surround yourself with colleagues and agency partners who are heavily entrenched in your category? The predictable result: category competitors start to look too much alike. Yes, if you pay really close attention (as these marketers certainly do), there are differences to be discovered, but marketers should never overestimate the real-life interest level of their customers.

In the end, category focus and intense competition tend to work against difference.

Yes, make your product or service better than your competitor's, but in ways that actually matter to your customer. Start from difference, be guided by that difference, and strive mightily to deliver that difference in a way that your audience will find better.

You are not just trying to be better; you are trying to create "differentiated advantage."

When you're working from difference, creative disruption becomes much easier to achieve.

If you haven't already, read *Blue Ocean Strategy*, by Renée Mauborgne and W. Chan Kim. They describe this phenomenon eloquently. To summarize, we have a tendency to get locked into "red oceans," fighting each other, glorying in the intense competition and turning the water red with our attacks. Instead we should search out "blue," unoccupied oceans, standing apart from traditional competition because we have become a category of one.

In other words, while it's important to be competitive, competition is actually bad for business.

In so many ways, we're addicted to and rewarded for traditional competition. Most of our marketplace performance measures are competition based. We liken this competition to war, wisely quoting Carl von Clausewitz and Sun Tzu along the way. It's easy to lock in on a competitor and the singular objective of playing the game better than they do. But how do brands really win?

Let's look at "challenger brands"—smaller brands that go head-to-head with a dominant market leader. David versus Goliath is a compelling story. But how do the underdogs of the business world win? By studying the market leaders, then doing something completely different. Challenger brands win the game by changing the rules.

The political scientist Ivan Arreguín-Toft recently looked at every war fought in the past two hundred years between strong and weak combatants. He analyzed conflicts in which the strong were at least ten times as powerful as the weak. Not surprisingly, the strong won in 71.5 percent of the cases. But when the underdog acknowledged their weakness and chose an unconventional strategy, the weaker combatant's winning percentage went from 29 percent to

64 percent. When underdogs do something different, they win the majority of the time.

Sure, it's important to understand the rules. Understand the operating principles in your category. Uncover the implicit assumptions that have guided category behavior. Then break the rules in a meaningful, culturally noisy way. Change the game. Find your blue ocean. Do different.

DIFFERENCE MAY DEMAND WEAKNESS.

To be truly great at something, so focused that you are uniquely associated with it, you will have to tolerate weakness in other areas. Apple makes elegant products, but their prices are high. Volvo is safe but boring. Southwest Airlines offers lower prices, but travelers cannot choose their seats in advance. And so on. This apparent weakness is tough for marketers, but I think most customers inherently understand and expect this sort of trade-off. Further, I think most brands spend way too much time trying to fix weaknesses, and not enough time leveraging their unique identifiers.

Of course, a weakness that is a deal breaker for your customer has to be addressed. An expensive, elegantly designed computer that regularly crashes? That's not going to fly. But what about other weaknesses? What is the opportunity cost of trying to fix everything you don't do well? What if you focused instead on leveraging your differentiated strength to its fullest potential?

If something is really working hard for you, especially if it has the potential to uniquely identify your brand, then ask yourself, *Have we placed a big enough bet behind it? How extreme could we make this advantage? What would it look like if we pushed it to its limits? How might we extend and deepen this advantage, breathing its essence into everything we do?*

In my experience, it's much better to be great at one thing and poor at another than to be just good at both.

DIFFERENCE OF IDEAS, NOT JUST BRANDS.

Inevitably, as someone thinks through a difference-based positioning strategy, they build some form of competitive map. Those who are a bit myopic will map only their current competitors. Those who are more forward looking will think through what that competitive set might look like tomorrow. But what if you thought of the marketplace as a battle of ideas rather than brands?

Ask yourself: *What are the ideas out there that can help me? What are the ideas that can hurt me? What are the ideas that will gain social currency? What are the ideas that will lose it?* Let's say you created a grid with these two axes—help versus hurt, and gain currency versus lose currency. Grid or no grid, the point is this: look at your market as a place of ideas rather than one of competitive brands, and see where this takes you.

Marketing is judo, not karate. Good marketing looks for ideas and beliefs that already exist (or can find a comfortable home) in the minds of the audience, then leverages the momentum of those ideas.

Karate is sometimes necessary, but it's a brave, expensive move. For example, when we thought Nike was a man's world, they managed to convince us they were also for women. When we saw Abercrombie as a tired brand for older people, they somehow convinced us they were young and sexy. (Sure, they later lost the script, but what an amazing perceptual shift.) Currently a strong cultural belief is killing big beer brands like Budweiser: the idea that craft beer is superior because of its handcrafted nature. What if I told you that Bud is better? What if I did blind taste tests (to remove the brand bias that clearly exists), and the majority of craft beer drinkers picked Bud? Would this new narrative gain currency, or would people dismiss the idea because it doesn't fit their beliefs? Maybe we'll find out someday.

Shifting your focus from competitive brands to cultural ideas will open up possibilities for difference-based marketing. Know the ideas that will gain currency, then leverage the momentum of those ideas, or know the ideas that can hurt you, and think through a solution of some kind. Either approach can yield difference, as either can lead you to an idea that becomes uniquely yours. Overall, just never lose track of the fact that you compete within a moving marketplace of ideas.

AS WE CAN ALL ATTEST, ANY IDIOT CAN BE DIFFERENT.

Make no mistake, there's smart difference and there's dumb difference. Dumb difference is difference for its own sake. Difference that is sort of painted on without actually wrestling with, and solving for, the underlying complexity. Difference that lacks competitive advantage, or that your audience just doesn't find compelling. Borrowed difference that isn't true to your product or has nothing whatsoever to do with your business strategy. As I learned early in my career, if you can just ignore the strategy, things suddenly get very easy. Dumb. Ineffective. Wasteful. But easy.

When it comes to marketing strategy (and perhaps life in general), simplicity exists on both sides of complexity. On the near side is naïve simplicity, which exists only because it has not yet acknowledged, understood, and solved for inherent complexities. Dumb difference is the byproduct of naïve simplicity. Then there is complexity, waiting to entice and trap the unwary. Yes, I know it's complicated, but your job is to make it simple. Only on the far side of the complexity trap will you find elegant simplicity, which addresses all that complexity with a singular solution. Elegant simplicity is the key to smart, differentiated strategy.

Put another way, strategy development is a form of pattern recognition: the ability to organize complex, relevant input in a way that reveals a pattern. A pattern that can yield a single, differentiated solution.

To have any hope of sensing that pattern, you need several sources of information, various angles, opposing perspectives. You need to weigh all of that complexity and process it through human minds in order to create unique insights. You need to separate the valuable, actionable insights from the background noise. As far as I know, a computer algorithm still can't do this (yet). This kind of pattern recognition requires an experienced and imaginative human brain, with both left and right sides actively working together.

This is the essence of smart difference: It addresses the pattern. It rings true to the complexity of relevant information. It makes intuitive sense to, and is a compelling force for, your audience. It is true to the product or service it represents. The deeper that difference sits in your business model and organizational culture, the more sustainable it will be.

THE SINGULAR INSIGHT.

A while back, our team made what I considered to be a brilliant strategic presentation to a client. We walked through the steps that would build the strategy, starting with defining the audience and then identifying the audience insights that would guide our thinking. At the end, I congratulated our team on a job well done, and we left the building.

A couple of months later I got a call from the client. Much to my dismay, she didn't want to talk about the strategy at all. Ultimately, though, the reason for her call was much more interesting.

Apparently, a young product designer had attended our presentation that day. For all I know he napped through most it, but a specific comment we made about an audience segment got him thinking. A creative seed had been planted, completely inadvertently. To make a long story short, the company launched the designer's brainchild, which has become a ridiculously successful global line of products. While we'd love to take credit for this success, we knew not what we did.

Yes, the pattern recognition that creates strategy is important, but we must also watch for singular insights that can activate a line of thinking that leads to something completely unique. Always keep your eyes open for things you can't quite see.

DIFFERENCE IN STRATEGY, AND DIFFERENCE IN TACTICS.

So far I have focused on difference as the engine room of all great positioning strategies, yet difference can be just as important tactically, where the battle is to stand out from all the executional noise in the marketplace. Strategic or tactical, the same rules apply: you need to stand out in a way that uniquely fits the differentiated position you are trying to occupy.

The goal is tactical difference born of strategic difference.

Put another way, your strategic difference sets the stage, but your audience sees tactics, not strategy. The right differentiated strategy will make it easier to create unique tactical expression, but the strategy can't do the work on its own. Your tactics have to fit your position, and they have to be disruptive in their own right to get your unique position noticed.

It's now early 2021, and we've all been dealing with the COVID-19 pandemic in our own way (clearly mine is to hunker down at home and write). Though it seems like a lifetime, it was only a year ago that we watched the Super Bowl, the ultimate stage for some of the most sophisticated marketers and ad agencies in the United States. When the game began, I had one question in mind: Would we see difference, or much of the same? By the end, my question had changed: Where did difference go? Has it been slowly leaving the building since Apple 1984?

Since then I've been trying hard to come up with recent examples of smart tactical difference. So far, I've seen one standout in 2020: Burger King's moldy Whopper. "The beauty of real food is that it gets ugly." Look it up. They did the exact opposite of what any sane person would expect.

Setting 2020 aside, I spent way too much time watching 2019's ad campaigns, and I'm ready to present awards to a few brands: Best Ambush goes to Aviation Gin for spoofing that awful Peloton ad. Hands down, no one close. Best Cinematography goes to Jif Peanut Butter (believe it or not), along with Lacoste and Apple (always easy to believe). Best Overall goes to Nike, partly because they're just really good and partly because Wieden+Kennedy is too. But my Highest DQ Praise is reserved for Halo Top and Splenda. Halo Top completely flipped the script on ice cream (search "ice cream for adults"), and Splenda gave a simple story an unexpected twist to call attention to its key difference (search "grow your own").

Ice cream and sweetener as beacons of difference—who would've guessed? If they can do it, we can too.

Differentiated positioning strategy sets the stage for truly unique and disruptive tactical execution. It's a difference multiplier: differentiated position x differentiated disruption. If you're a marketing geek like me, you can tell when marketing teams and their communication agencies have found their groove. Like difference itself, it's still a disturbingly rare phenomenon, but it's really fun to watch.

The value of finding this difference multiplier for your business can be in the billions. In chapter 11, I'll provide more examples of differentiated, disruptive tactics in action—campaigns that, quite literally, changed the future of a brand and business.

IT'S SIMPLE, BUT IT'S NOT EASY.

Creating smart difference is simple. Procedurally, it's just two steps:

> Step 1: List the ways in which your "thing" (person, place, idea, product, company) is different.

> Step 2: Select the difference that contains the greatest competitive advantage and audience appeal.

Complete these two steps, and there you have it: a very short list of differentiated advantages.

One of my favorite illustrations of this simple approach comes from some really fun positioning work we did for Warner Brothers many years ago. We looked at superheroes as an exercise in brand positioning, assessing the current state of their brands. For instance, Batman has many interesting and unique equities, but according to research with kids around the world, his single most compelling difference turns out to be this: Batman started with a purpose. Other superheroes were generally born with or given their powers, then they went through some sort of angst-filled evolution as they decided how they would put those powers to use. Batman, however, decided to become a superhero, then he acquired the skills and gear necessary to fulfill that purpose. It turns out kids love this difference, probably because they see possibility for themselves in it.

The act of positioning Batman also shows that, even with a strong and compelling point of difference, cultural context can be critically important. Kids identified with Batman's unique narrative, which we shorthanded to "From purpose comes power." However, they saw him as dark and lonely. He had no real friends, and he lived in a cold mansion with an ancient butler. They knew he must be rich, but they didn't know how he got his money (they assumed it was given to him). Worst of all, in the eyes of this young audience, Batman was really old—maybe even forty! Warner Brothers quickly shifted this cultural context, or character backstory, across all of the products they managed directly. As luck would have it, a brilliant director named Christopher Nolan soon came along, very interested in making a film about Batman's origin story, and the Caped Crusader was reborn.

Batman is truly different, in a way that is very compelling to kids. We just needed to focus on that difference and change the cultural context through which it operated. Incidentally, Superman also has a critical cultural weakness, and it's not kryptonite. It turns out that Superman is too perfect. Too strong. Too powerful. You can only create so many plotlines that involve bad guys weakening him with kryptonite. From a storytelling perspective, Superman's strength is his weakness.

Finding your difference probably won't be as easy as finding Batman's, but the steps are essentially the same: list your differences, then choose the one with the greatest advantage and appeal.

As you'll see, when it comes to difference, the difficulty is not in the process, but in the doing. The difficulty is in calibrating that intuitive leap, then having the courage and conviction required to see it through. Easy process. Tough application.

DIFFERENCE ALWAYS BEGINS WITH THE THING.

Difference starts with the product, service, place, person, or idea we are selling. If the thing itself contains differentiated advantage, we're way ahead in the marketing race. If the thing isn't unique in a compelling way, we start at a significant—sometimes insurmountable—disadvantage. This has always been true, but never more so than today. In our technology-enabled world, customers' ability to compare products quickly on their ever-present smartphones greatly reduces the odds of a weak, undifferentiated product surviving. Reduces those odds to about zero.

Yes, uniquely great things can fail if positioned poorly. Yes, weak and undifferentiated things can prosper through great positioning. But if you're a bettor, don't place any of your hard-earned money against either of these outcomes. Great positioning strategy is additive. It makes the weak stronger and the strong stronger still—but there is absolutely nothing like starting with a great thing.

A highly differentiated position is absolutely no guarantee of success. The truth always wins out, and the truth can be found only in your customer's experience. If at all possible, your differentiated position should emerge organically from that customer experience. At the end of the day, the quality and essential nature of what we're selling will always be more important than the way we position it.

While the strongest and fastest won't always win the race—that's definitely the way to bet.

Apple doesn't win because they're masters of differentiated brand positioning (though they most certainly are); they win because they make unique products—elegant responses to the technological complexity they artfully keep in the background. Dyson didn't come out of nowhere to capture our imagination because of positioning or message, but because Jim Dyson spent countless hours perfecting his vacuum cleaner. Many years ago now, my colleagues and I pledged our travel stays to Westin, not because of clever positioning but because of the Westin experience—heavenly beds, great pillows, a great customer loyalty program, and access to gym gear.

Quality of customer experience seals the deal. No matter what we are selling, we need to map out that entire experience and find ways to make it as uniquely compelling as is economically sensible. Yes, our positioning strategy must be difference based, but if our "thing" doesn't truly pay off that differentiated position, then time, transparency, and competition will doom it to failure.

Do you remember TV Guide? Ever heard of it? The brand began as a weekly print magazine featuring a schedule of television programs and some related articles. Eventually they added an on-screen TV schedule that scrolled perpetually. So if you missed the program listing for channel 2, you had to wait for the guide to roll through all the other channels until channel 2 came around again.

Well, once upon a time (yes, it really was that long ago), when I was president of strategy at Sterling Brands, TV Guide asked us to come up with a positioning strategy. At first I thought, *Come on—it's a guide to television. Isn't the position pretty damn obvious?* The position was great—different, compelling, meaningful. But it was placed in service to products that were woefully out of date—an analog response to a rapidly digitizing entertainment world. Worse, the brand still defined TV in traditional terms, rather than extending it across a much broader definition of content. We set out to remedy that.

In our presentation to TV Guide, when I identified their position as "guide" and explained the rapidly growing need for a guide in today's entertainment world, they loved me. When I told them they had to radically change the way they guided viewers, the room suddenly went cold. I soldiered on, illustrating how they could maximize their position, developing a broader content range and a more digitally driven product portfolio. But I'd gone from hero to villain in a matter of minutes. To my surprise, TV Guide was not going to change.

TV Guide effectively went out of business. Not because the world didn't want a unique guide to content, but because that guide refused to do the hard work necessary to evolve with the times. They had the position, but their "thing" couldn't make the grade. In general, bet on the great thing over the great position.

WHAT IF THE THING ISN'T THAT DIFFERENT?

Apple, Netflix, ESPN, Disney, Nike, Walmart, Airbnb, Nike—these clearly defined, highly focused propositions have generated unique, compelling products and services. A marketer's dream. Of course, this level of difference is relatively rare. Most marketers work at the opposite end of the spectrum, creating a differentiating point of view around a product that isn't actually all that unique. This is where we marketers really earn our keep.

As a case in point, look at Dove—at one point, a bar of soap worth about $400 million globally. Dove wanted to introduce a line of face-care products, but none had the inherent differentiated advantage that might make a marketer's life a bit easier. My business partner, Alpa Pandya, worked with the brand team and uncovered a potentially differentiating insight—real women were sick and tired of a beauty category that looked like it cared only about tall, thin, scantily clad supermodels. Once our team recognized the "problem," they asked the question: Would women appreciate it if Dove championed the point of view that real beauty is about celebrating one's uniqueness? Particularly in the beauty category, this would be a truly provocative, uniquely compelling point of view. The response among women was a highly enthusiastic yes.

Through consistency, intelligent product extension, and some great marketing communication around the world, Dove is now working its way to $5 billion in sales.

The Dove strategy had an incredible outcome, but it was risky: the compelling point of difference was only skin-deep. Because it was purely a marketing construct, competitors could have copied it a week later. They didn't, and with time and a consistently high-quality marketing effort, Dove has come to own the idea. But ownership wasn't inevitable. Dove had to commit to the idea and run with it, into the great unknown.

That's the thing about difference—it's different, and different feels like a risk. Whether embedded in your product or created by your marketing team, difference contains risk. At this point you know why I believe taking the leap is imperative, so now let's see if the science of difference can help us reduce that sense of risk.

"It is beneath human dignity to lose one's individuality and become a mere cog in the machine."
—Mahatma Gandhi

CHAPTER 2

THE SCIENCE OF DIFFERENCE

"A ship in harbor is safe, but that is not what ships are built for."
—John A. Shedd

Differentiation is critically important to marketing success. You're probably not going to find many people who would argue with you on this point, as it's always been an accepted part of marketing lore. But when it comes time to actually do different, you're likely to meet some resistance from people who prefer that comfort zone called the gray middle. Fortunately, you've got science on your side. Years ago, Young & Rubicam spent the money, built the database, and proved the importance of difference through something they called Brand Asset Valuator (BAV). When I worked at Y&R, I loved BAV, not so much because of its great information, but because it made an incredibly persuasive, data-driven case for difference.

More recently, a company called BERA has perfected a more real-time diagnostic measurement of this thing we call differentiation. Like Brand Asset Valuator and others, BERA has done a lot of financial modeling of difference, as brands with high differenti-ation have been shown to outperform the Standard & Poor's (S&P) average. In fact, 96 percent of the "most loved" brands in BERA were shown to outperform the S&P 500.

BERA measures several key brand attributes weekly across four thousand brands and two hundred categories. In total, they survey one million American consumers each year. Why?

Part of the answer lies in the fact that brand measures such as difference are much more volatile than we like to think. For years, marketers tended to view hard business measures, such as volume numbers and market share, as responsive and volatile. At the same time, they viewed brand measures as soft and not responsive to short-term changes in the conditions around them. Turns out this perspective was born more of how things were measured than how things actually work in the real world.

Brand measures were viewed as long-term and slow changing, so they were measured annually, sometimes through dangerously misleading financial metrics, like the valuations provided annually by certain mainstream business publications. To be clear, financial metrics can be lagging indicators of brand health, often artificially inflated in ways that can actually harm the business in the longer run. Of course, financial measures are a critically important report card for a business. At times they will correlate with differentiated advantage, but they should not be confused with the future health of your brand and business.

With BERA, brand metrics can be measured weekly if needed, and it turns out they are much more volatile than we historically liked to believe. For me at least, the most important thing BERA does is measure four key brand-building dimensions:

- uniqueness
- meaning

- familiarity
- regard

To simplify, BERA combines all four measures into a single "brand love" score, but for our use here, it's more important to look at each measure independently.

This will shock you: I think uniqueness is the key measure. Actually, the science makes this clear, so we're well past opinions at this point. For example, in a cross-category analysis, "uniqueness" has been shown to correlate highly with a consumer's willingness to pay a price premium, giving us a clear indication of how a brand can lessen pricing sensitivity and improve profitability. Difference drives pricing power and overall brand strength.

Again, any idiot can be different, so a brand's uniqueness must be personally meaningful to its audience. Combined with meaningfulness, we get "meaningful uniqueness"—and our leading indicator. Leading indicators are rare, and therefore worth their weight in gold, because they signal things to come. When your meaningful uniqueness increases, good things will happen, and when it declines there is well-founded cause for concern.

More traditionally tracked measures such as "familiarity" and "regard" were found to be lagging indicators. These measures (the ones we seem to spend so much time and money tracking) degrade slowly and can be artificially maintained through marketing expenditure or price discounting. So by the time they start to fall off, your company might already be in a ton of trouble.

When leading indicators exceed lagging indicators, a brand has positive momentum, but when lagging indicators are higher, its best days are behind it unless something changes.

Just for fun (and to exercise a deep personal well of regret), consider Hillary Clinton and Donald Trump as they neared the 2016 election. Both had familiarity-score percentile rankings in the high 90s. Clinton was well ahead of Trump on regard and meaningfulness. But Trump outscored her 72 to 26 on difference. Lesson learned?

A FINANCIAL ANALYSIS FROM A FINANCIAL DUMMY.

I started college as a math major, but I ignored MBA advisers who encouraged me to go into finance, as I fell in love with marketing. There has been a lot of very complex financial analysis done on BAV and BERA data, and you're about to get a summary of it, as filtered through my nonfinancial, used-to-be-good-at-math brain.

The bottom line is that highly differentiated brands perform better than poorly differentiated brands on every relevant financial measure. If you're willing to just accept this at face value, I thank you for your trust and suggest that you skip the following analysis.

If you're still reading, here we go. This is my layman's summary, informed by a *CFO Magazine* article from January 2018.

The analysis was done over three years, on 160 publicly owned, single-brand companies (single brand because this enables calculation that uses brand and publicly available financial measures). For our purposes here, I'll use the numbers from an analysis that looked at the ratio of leading indicators (meaningful uniqueness) to lagging indicators (familiarity and regard). They separated companies into two groups, comparing those with a ratio greater than the median to those with a ratio less than the median. Unfortunately, they didn't create more significant differences by comparing top quartile to bottom quartile, but you'll get the analytical drift.

Here's what they found. Average annual sales growth for those companies with a ratio greater than the median was 4 percent, which was 0.7 percent greater than those with a ratio below the median. This is actually smaller than I would have expected, but let's again keep in mind that the two groupings are only separated by a very thin line called the median. If we compared companies at opposite ends of the curve, the differences would obviously be much more pronounced.

When you look at profit-driven dimensions, the differences are greater. On one such metric, called residual cash earnings (RCE), the above-median group recorded an RCE margin of 11.4 percent, while the below-median group came in at 9.5 percent. This essentially means that for each dollar in sales growth, the above-median group delivered about 20 percent more RCE.

Above-median companies delivered an EBITDA (earnings before interest, tax, depreciation, and amortization) multiple of 13.2x, versus 10.4x. This means that for each dollar in EBITDA, the above-median companies delivered 27 percent more enterprise value than the below-median companies.

Building difference leads to significantly greater financial returns. In other words, difference is very good for business, even if you're the CFO. So much so that pre-BERA, a prominent Wall Street company even considered building a fund around highly differentiated brands, as measured by Y&R's Brand Asset Valuator.

End of me pretending I know what I'm talking about in the world of finance.

DIFFERENCE IS CATEGORY AGNOSTIC.

When you imagine the classic growth curve of a brand through the dimensions measured by BERA, you pinpoint a critical challenge in marketing.

When a new product, service, or company is "born," its task is to be as meaningfully unique as possible—highly different and compelling, but to a relatively small group of people. These people, and the uniqueness of the new brand, will help it build its audience, but only to a point. Getting to this point means you created something that feels meaningfully unique to your audience, and you are to be congratulated—but the next step is just as tough, if not tougher.

The next step requires a truly extraordinary marketing strategy: you need to build your audience without losing your difference. Think of it this way: You've gained altitude based on difference. Now how can you hold that altitude while covering a much broader landscape?

Being truly different while appealing to a mass audience is extremely difficult. Most brands don't manage step one successfully—they just don't achieve the meaningful uniqueness needed to become a major player. Of those that are truly different, most achieve personal meaning only to a relatively small audience. Nothing wrong with this—they can be small, highly profitable niche players, but they will not achieve scale unless they can convince a mass market that their difference is personally meaningful. This is the kind of challenge that keeps marketing teams gainfully employed. How do you actually meet this challenge? We'll talk more about that in the chapters to come.

Meanwhile, as you push for difference, consider this: Your brand might look like best in class for its category—a veritable giant. But if the entire category lacks difference, you're actually just the tallest of the dwarves.

As a case in point, you might look at ESPN versus other sports-broadcasting brands. They rule. They dominate their competitive set. But then you realize that the average American adult spends 11.5 hours a day looking at a screen of some kind, an amazing statistic in its own right. ESPN is locked in an intense competition for a share of that viewing time, not just with sports-broadcasting brands, but also with incredibly strong entertainment brands such as Google, YouTube, Amazon, Netflix—and now ESPN's parent brand, Disney+. While BERA shows that ESPN is a very strong brand that dominates their in-category competition, it also reveals that they lag these powerful entertainment brands, all of which sit at the very top of the difference game. This picture stays the same, even when you focus the analysis on a sports-fan audience.

Difference is category agnostic. Because this is the way the world works for consumers, this is the only accurate way to look at your brand. No harm done if you take a category-specific look at your competitive set, but those who take only a category-specific approach risk creating a highly misleading picture.

To illustrate, here are a few interesting marketplace observations using BERA data.

As uniqueness is the acknowledged engine room of brand strength, I'll focus on uniqueness scores for now. A brand's uniqueness score simply represents the brand's percentile ranking against all four thousand brands within the database. Also, keep in mind that the audience used for this analysis is all adults, which will artificially inflate some scores and hurt others. You'd never do this in practice, but it will have to suffice for my purposes.

One more important point—these numbers are pre-COVID. The world has changed dramatically for all of us since then. It would be fascinating to look at the changes from pre- to post-COVID (if there is truly such a thing as "post"), but I'll leave that for someone else to report on.

With these disclaimers in place, for 2019 the top 15 most highly differentiated brands in America were:

1. Amazon   99.6
2. National Geographic   99.4
3. LEGO   99.3
4. Google   99.3
5. Pixar   99.2
6. YouTube   99.1
7. Reese's   98.7
8. M&M's   98.7

9.	Microsoft	98.5
10.	Discovery Channel	98.5
11.	History Channel	98.5
12.	Crayola	98.2
13.	Apple	98.0
14.	PBS	98.0
15.	Tesla	98.0

The ranking from number 1 to number 15 is somewhat irrelevant, as their uniqueness scores are all very strong. Several other brands sit just below 98, so this is just an interesting starter list. Still, note that every single one of these brands brings a unique point of view to the table. (Although I have to admit I wouldn't have expected Microsoft and Apple to be so close on uniqueness, but on reflection, neither brand has anyone who looks or feels anything like them.)

You might, quite rightly, observe that all these brands sit in inherently interesting categories. When I discussed some of them with a colleague, she called them the "sexy brands." I think difference is sexy, so I guess that's true, but we're missing something if we assume that only certain categories can house high difference scores. For example, USPS, PBS, Wikipedia, Vicks, Swiffer, Burt's Bees, Kit Kat, and Pringles all score over 95 on uniqueness.

And look at Crayola. No matter your category, uniqueness is possible.

DIFFERENTIATED BRANDS CREATE CULTURAL SHIFTS.

BERA data also reveals the impact of cultural shifts on leading (or formerly leading) brands. Spoiler alert: to make it across the river of change, you must be either the one who creates the change, or the one who takes earliest and fullest advantage of it.

For instance, the entertainment arena is seeing lots of interesting action these days, and that's where we find many of the strongest brands. Looking at the average scores for 2019, there's really not much space between these six:

- Amazon   99.6
- Disney   99.2
- Pixar   99.2
- YouTube   99.1
- Apple   98.1
- Netflix   97.7

As you saw in the top 15 list, these represent some of the strongest difference scores among the four thousand brands measured. Now let's compare them to more traditional broadcast brands:

- ABC   69.5
- CBS   62.9
- NBC   61.8

As you may have guessed, it's a tough road ahead for these broadcast brands. They've simply let too much time go by, wishfully focused on an out-of-date entertainment model. The situation is worse if you're a cable supplier, even if you try to change your name:

- Xfinity   28.2
- Comcast   10.3

It's hard to see how the cable operators avoid being relegated to simply becoming providers of high-speed internet access, which in many ways seems like the natural extension of their role in our viewing lives.

How about a comparison of the uniqueness score of Tesla (97.9) and General Motors (62.1)?

Or a comparison of Southwest Airlines (65.6) to the justifiably low scores of our other domestic airline brands, ranging from a high of 36 (Delta) to a low of 20.9 (United)?

When we compare Amazon (99.6) and Walmart (84.3) to the Gap Inc. portfolio, we get a glimpse of things to come in the mainstream apparel market:

- Old Navy   61.6
- Gap   31.2
- Banana Republic   24.8

While on apparel, I'd be remiss if I didn't give a shout-out to one of America's most resilient brands, Levi Strauss. They managed a uniqueness score of 88.7 in 2019. This brand weathered a bad management storm incredibly well, and currently seems to be in much safer and smarter hands.

Kudos also to Dove, which remains the second most highly differentiated brand in a highly cluttered beauty category, largely because their uniquely meaningful "real beauty" position identified, leveraged, and perhaps even helped create a cultural shift.

A once highly differentiated brand landscape, bottled water, has fallen on hard times. People seem to have realized that plastic isn't good for the environment and have rediscovered that thing in their kitchen called a tap. Across all sparkling and still water brands, the average uniqueness score is only 34.

Looking at a different beverage category, as a marketer it hurts to see the state of the beer category in the United States. The mainstream domestic brands I grew up with all score single digits on uniqueness. Despite much smaller distribution footprints, every single craft beer measured scores higher than these brands, as did all but three imported brands. As a new and developing category, every single FMB brand (flavored malt beverages, such as Mike's Hard Lemonade) outscores the domestic beers.

How about people? Tom Hanks checks in with the highest celebrity score, at 98.7, followed closely by Stephen King (98.6) and Dwayne "The Rock" Johnson (97.1). Donald Trump still checks in with a reasonable uniqueness score of 68.5, though this is down about 10 points from his preelection numbers.

All of these brands are considered highly unique by American adults, but what about the other end of the spectrum? In terms of celebrity, it didn't look good toward the end of 2019 for Khloe and Kim Kardashian, both sitting at 0.1 difference scores. These incredibly effective builders of the content-free Kardashian brand have made a fortune, and hats off to them, but the future doesn't look so bright. For very different reasons, Matt Lauer is right there with them. Joining them with scores of less than 2 are Justin Bieber, Kanye West, Megyn Kelly, and Sean Combs. Who knows? Maybe by the time you read this, you'll have to google these one-time household names to find out who they are.

More commercially, the bottom of the barrel features the aforementioned host of domestic beer brands, Motel 6, Dish TV, and Abercrombie & Fitch. Welcome to the "Oh yeah, what happened to those brands?" portion of the discussion. When you find yourself pushing for difference, share these brands and their data with the people blocking your path. The numbers will speak for themselves.

LET'S TALK FORWARD MOMENTUM.

In BERA terms, brands with the most "forward momentum" are those with the biggest positive gap between lagging and leading indicators. I've selected a few representative brands:

- CamelBak   59.4 (positive percentage
                               point delta)
- Method   54.5
- The Honest Company   51.5
- Seventh Generation   49.8
- Monkey Shoulder   47.8
- Around the Horn   47.3
- Nest   46.7
- Lagunitas Brewing
  Company   46.4
- TaskRabbit   44.4
- Salesforce   44.2

Granted, some of these brands have a high difference between lagging and leading indicators because of low awareness and therefore consideration, but the list is interesting, nonetheless. In theory, this is the kind of list you should be picking stocks from, though by the time you read this it will be dangerously out of date.

Stock portfolios aside, it's interesting to see the broad range of categories represented. For those who don't know, Monkey Shoulder is a scotch whiskey, and there were several other scotch whiskey brands on this list, so I assume the category is surging. (Given my own Scottish heritage, I believe this trend is long overdue.) TaskRabbit is an interesting inclusion, as it was recently acquired by IKEA and seems to be faltering. It does have relatively low awareness, and its justifiably high difference score is driving this sense of forward momentum. Lastly, hats off to Salesforce, showing a level of forward momentum you just don't expect from business-to-business companies of its size.

Now what about the flip side of this equation—brands with the largest negative difference between leading and lagging indicators? I'll select a few just to make the point:

- Diet Pepsi   53.3 (negative percentage point delta)
- DirecTV   49.6
- WWE   44.3
- MTV   44.0
- Smirnoff   42.0
- Heineken   40.9
- T-Mobile   39.1
- Mary Kay   37.5
- Banana Republic   35.8
- Bloomingdale's   35.6
- Twitter   30.7

Diet Pepsi is interesting in that Diet Coke also lacks a sense of forward momentum, though the situation isn't nearly as dire. Both parent cola brands are significantly outperforming their offspring at the moment, as consumers are selecting beverages that feel more "naturally" low in calories. Banana Republic has already lived two lives, and it has been in desperate need of a third for quite some time now. First Banana Republic was weird but different, then it was normal and not at all different. If there is an imaginative third path forward, they'd better hurry up and find it. I will continue to think there's a solution for MTV, as long as there are young people whose interests differ from older people's, but this brand may just be out of runway. Personally, I think T-Mobile has tried mightily to differentiate itself from its highly undifferentiated but larger competitors. But as long as this market is driven by such heavy, unrelenting price communication, it'll be tough to see difference through all of that promotional category noise.

COVID-19 crisis aside, the Bloomingdale's problem is obvious, and probably insurmountable. In general, this shift in retailing is fascinating to watch from the outside, but really painful to experience on the inside. In the good old days, one retailer had to convince you that their store was better than that of a competitor. This was a fair competitive arena, where the shopping effort was roughly the same, and it came down to who was most uniquely compelling. Today the onus is on all physical retailers to prove that the effort required to get into their store is worth it, given that we can stay in our slippers and shop on our computers to our hearts' content. Today's physical retailer has to convince us to spend two of our most precious resources—our time and money—to shop in their store. This is obviously a tough sell, and it's only going to get tougher.

As a hopeless optimist, I'd argue that all of these weak-brand situations could be turned around, and that it might be a lot of fun to take that challenge on. While there is such a thing as a point of no return, that point is really a combination of cultural irrelevance and financial discretion. In other words, some brands just aren't worth saving, even by hopeless optimists like me.

DIFFERENCE BUILDS BUSINESSES AND BRANDS.

Okay, enough science. Hopefully all of this data is interesting, and perhaps some of it is even surprising, but this wasn't really the objective. The point of all of this was to get past the rhetoric of people like me, and past the expected parade of case studies, to prove the importance of difference scientifically. There are other tracking studies that could be used and lots more data to be perused, but the basic point is undeniable: difference builds businesses and brands.

Without question, having, finding, or creating difference is essential to success. As a marketer of anything, no matter how anxiety producing difference might be, avoiding the risk inherent to forging a differentiated path is actually the greatest risk of all. The choice is clear: find that path or lose yourself among the many who walk the well-beaten track. Make no mistake, over time, a lack of difference will make life extremely difficult. Sooner, not later, lack of difference will mean lack of business.

If you are a brand marketer, you must track your difference. I don't care how you track it; just do it. The world has generously handed you a leading indicator—ignore it at your (and your company's) peril.

I've regaled you with my opinions on difference and bludgeoned you with data that proves its importance. Now let's look at some tangible illustrations of people, businesses, and brands that have won by playing the difference game.

"You have to be odd to be number one."

—Dr. Seuss

CHAPTER 3

WHAT'S REALLY
GOING ON HERE?

*"Nobody can be exactly like me. Sometimes
even I have trouble doing it."*

—Tallulah Bankhead

Let's return to my favorite place, the land of opinion, and take a closer look at that central question: If we can all agree that difference builds brands and businesses, why the hell are we so afraid of it?

Why do we nod our heads when someone like me mentions the importance of difference, but later ask for examples of people who have done something similar in the past, in order to reassure us that we're not about to drive off a cliff? Why do we lionize those who are truly different—Richard Branson, Steve Jobs, Bill Gates, Jeff Bezos, Mark Zuckerberg, Marc Benioff, Larry Ellison—but not act more like them? Why do we talk a good difference game, then fail to play that game out?

Clearly there are some major difference-dampening forces at work here—institutional, social, psychological, and biological. We'll talk about those in part II. For now, let's see how fear of difference shows up in business.

Back in college, many of us started to spread our wings, imagining the radical ways we would change the world. But when graduation came, especially if we walked out the door with an MBA in hand, we took that big company job and quickly learned that those who fit in progressed faster and further. If we had the urge to do something truly different, odds are our company nipped that in the bud pretty quickly.

When we are young and junior, we are not really paid to think; we are paid to analyze. In a meeting, senior leaders can say "I think," while juniors—if they speak at all—are generally limited to "the data shows." Over time, for many of us, this will act to dull our DQ. If you accept the recurring idea that difference is created rather than constructed, at some point the data must be used to fuel an intuitive leap of some kind. But our company is telling us that this is not our role. We are paid to support and analyze, not to think and create.

To make matters worse, difference has no track record. By definition, difference has few case studies or analogs to point to. Difference requires putting all bets behind your one big shot, while non-difference-based decisions are generally smaller and more easily reversed. Not to mention, when we push for something totally unique, our coworkers and supervisors may think we're crazy. (At least once, we'll probably agree with them.)

In short, the business and personal risk of true difference is high.

Worst-case scenario? We could fail. In fact, if we're a technology startup, our company's odds of success are roughly one in a hundred. If we're a packaged goods company, life is a bit safer. New packaged goods products tend to be more incremental in nature, but they still fail 85 percent of the time. In other words, if we're doing something truly original, the odds are not in our favor.

When we fail by taking the expected route, the familiar path, our failure is softer. Less visible. More understandable to those around us. More incremental and, therefore, more readily course-corrected. When we do something truly different, however, we risk highly visible, possibly monumental failure. The kind of failure people will write about. The kind of failure that gets people fired or sends them to bankruptcy court.

But—and it's a huge but—when we do something truly different and succeed, we succeed fully. We build case studies that people emulate. We build iconic businesses and brands. We create industries where none existed. We change the future. We rock.

There is no "like" in a difference-based strategy. You may hate it or you may love it, but it's hard to be iffy about difference. Done well, difference creates a very clear and thick line between the idea you stand for and an idea everyone else stands for. This is exactly the sense of choice you should be building in the marketplace, but it's definitely not for the faint of heart.

When I talk about difference as a way to create a clear choice in the marketplace, people get worried. I can almost see them thinking, *But what if I create a clear choice and the customer doesn't choose me?* I understand the hesitation. Choice is black or white, and you need to be really confident that your money is on the right color.

I don't mean to scare you. I honestly believe that not taking a risk is the biggest risk of all. Creating difference—successfully—will make life so much easier. It will make you richer, more famous, and better looking than those who plod along without creating it. Difference may be a bit scary, but it's also just much—more—fun.

Still not convinced? We'll see how you feel at the end of the book.

Getting back to ground level, let's consider three forms of difference: the somewhat legendary startup heroes, those who have uncovered difference inside a business that's already "in flight," and those who, lacking any tangible difference, created a differentiated point of view. We'll take a deeper dive into these topics later in the book, but for now we'll use them to organize the discussion.

STARTUPS ARE THE HOME OF FOLK HEROES.

Let's look at some stories about the creation of difference. Here I'll focus on differentiated businesses that have been both entrepreneurial in nature and earthshaking in outcome, as they set the bar for the rest of us. These businesses' high visibility makes them an easy reference point for most of us, but scale is not really the issue. As we'll discuss, niche is not a four-letter word, and many huge businesses started as small-niche players. If you have a truly differentiated idea that an audience finds compelling, you will succeed. If that audience stays small, you will own a nice home and drive a fast car. If that audience is huge, you will change the world. As a consultant who has done neither, I salute all of you and suggest that, while scale can differ wildly, the basic ingredients of differentiated entrepreneurship are exactly the same:

Nerves of Steel + Obsessive Focus + a Unique and Compelling Idea

=

Differentiated Entrepreneurship

In the land of the entrepreneur—a land filled with dreamers and pioneers—difference is built from the ground up. Our startup folk heroes have created something out of nothing, through sheer will and the ability to convince others to follow. These alphas teamed with a small group of people who shared their vision, who hired a larger group, and so on, until that vision was felt less viscerally and more intellectually by a much larger organization.

When I think of these massively different companies, I think of Peter Thiel and his "zero to one" construct. As he says in *Zero to One: Notes on Startups, or How to Build the Future*:

> Doing what we already know how to do takes the world from 1 to *n*, adding more of something familiar. But every time we create something new, we go from 0 to 1. The act of creation is singular, as is the moment of creation, and the result is something fresh and strange.

In this book, Thiel also wrote one of my favorite sentences: "Every business is successful exactly to the extent that it does something others cannot."

Not surprisingly, I love these thoughts (and how well they're articulated). Thiel views "1 to *n*" as a horizontal movement involving copying or iterating things that already work. "Zero to 1" is a completely different, vertical movement resulting in something truly new.

Those who have created zero-to-one-style companies are completely unique people who built something out of nothing, usually in the face of massive doubt and seemingly impossible odds. As Winston Churchill himself said, "Kites rise high against the wind, not with it." Because they number among the 1 percent who succeeded, these entrepreneurs are famous. Maybe not Kim Kardashian famous, but famous nonetheless. When I think of people like this, I think of that amazing 1997 Apple campaign from TBWA\Chiat\Day advertising, titled "Think Different":

> Here's to the crazy ones.
> The misfits. The rebels. The troublemakers.

> The round pegs in the square holes.
> The ones who see things differently.
> . . .
> Because the people who are crazy enough to
>   think they can change the world, are the
>   ones who do.[1]

Let's look at a few of those "crazy ones." At least to most people who would pick up a book like this, their stories are well known, but here's my take on them:

Steve Jobs was truly different. You could love him. You could hate him. You could love and hate him, but only the least opinionated, most uninvolved among us lacked a point of view. The best thing was that Jobs really didn't care how others felt; he was just doing his thing. He was following the beat of a unique internal rhythm. He followed it to success. He followed it to failure. He followed it to ugly depths and to ridiculous heights. If any single business leader epitomized difference, it was Jobs. He created a unique, once-in-several-lifetimes company. At one point he had built the most valuable brand we'd ever known. We love to use his name and his company, but 99.999 percent of us lack the nerve to follow in his footsteps.

Bill Gates is also different. His company was so boring compared to Apple that we scoffed at his blandness, but Gates created something out of nothing. He was a pioneer. When the rest of us would've sold our company to IBM for millions at the ripe old age of twenty-five, he licensed his software instead. What massive self-belief. Even now, after building this incredible company called Microsoft, he is taking a completely unique path forward: spending massive amounts of money to save the world. (Clearly, this man

---

1.   "Think Different," Apple advertising campaign, 1997. Script by Rob Siltanen, et al.

lacks ambition.) Like Jobs, Gates follows his own rhythm. Perhaps his drummer isn't as cool as Steve Jobs's was, but the beat is every bit as unique.

I once made a presentation to Microsoft's marketing team, at a time when Apple's hype was particularly high and, due to marketplace criticism, Microsoft's team was racked with self-doubt. Because my company worked with "trend forward" brands, I was asked to speak about ways Microsoft could be more "cool." My first slide stated, essentially: "If you have to ask someone like me how to do it, you will never, ever be cool." The point of that presentation applies to our purposes here: Microsoft didn't need to be "cool like Apple." They needed to be unique in a way that was completely true to who they were, then find the confidence to let the marketplace decide if their difference was compelling.

"Cool" is a marketplace response, not a stimulus. Rather than follow the sort of stimulus presented by Steve Jobs and Apple, Microsoft needed to present and celebrate a different yet equally unique face—the face of a software geek—which, as a brand, is who they actually were. While we knew Steve was cooler than Bill, we also needed to stop and consider that Bill would probably have beaten Steve's ass at chess.

Think of it this way: Peter Parker was a nerdy kid who was bitten by a spider, became a superhero, and got the girl of his dreams. In the early days of this movie franchise, Spider-Man was unbeatable, largely because of these unique ingredients and how both kids and adults personally identified with them. Bill Gates is Peter Parker. Bill Gates beats Steve Jobs at chess. Bill Gates is really, really cool.

Just to entwine these two huge figures more, one could argue that as someone who clearly saw the potential of Apple fairly early on, Bill Gates was essential to Jobs's Apple turnaround. For his own reasons, Gates invested in Apple in 1997, saving the company from bankruptcy. Here was his completely honest and accurate take on Jobs's company: "To create a new standard, it takes something that's not just a little bit different; it takes something that's really new and really captures people's imagination, and the Macintosh, of all the machines I've ever seen, is the only one that meets that standard."

To shift gears, **Travis Kalanick** founded Uber. Based on published reports, Mr. Kalanick sounds like an ass. I've never met him, so I can't offer a firsthand opinion, but I will say, when it comes to doing different, he's my kind of ass. Travis Kalanick and his partner cofounded a company that has proven life changing, totally unprecedented, and completely unique. The way he built Uber lacked a decent moral compass at times, but the company's difference factor is high. A few of us might have dreamt of ride sharing, but dreams are easy; reality is so much harder. In the words of Warren Buffet, "Predicting rain doesn't count; building arks does." Uber was a massive, game-changing, culture-shifting idea that took incredible will and perseverance to make real. Most of us, me included, would have folded under the pressure, but Kalanick did not. Yes, there seems to be reason to dislike this guy, but can't we also admire his willingness to chart a completely unique course, then see it through no matter the resistance, no matter the length of the odds? Maybe this is admitting ethical weakness, but I'm okay with calling him an ass while also congratulating him on an amazing, odds-defying feat.

Reed Hastings and **Marc Randolph** created Netflix, which, with benefit of hindsight, is a fascinating exercise in difference. The original idea was to sell or rent DVDs online. A completely different and somewhat challenging idea for a couple of reasons, not the least of which was the fact that the future of the DVD was completely up in the air. Then they decided that selling was not unique or focused enough (Amazon was looming on the horizon), so they concentrated on renting. Renting itself wasn't different enough and carried a host of operational issues, so they created a completely unique subscription model. Finally, the physical subscription gave way to an equally unique streaming subscription, which for me represents one of the boldest moves in corporate American history.

From my admittedly biased perspective, Netflix displayed a pretty amazing and consistent pursuit of difference. Every time they approached a crossroads, they bravely opted for the more unique path forward. I think they might argue against the bravery point, as they're so highly driven by data. But I've seen enough brave, different, data-supported choices left on the table to have an immense respect for people who have the courage to make those decisions. Even with all the data support in the world, that leap off the cliff is incredibly scary.

All along, Netflix has been one step ahead. Sure, sometimes the step was a bit of a stumble, particularly early on when the learning curve was steep, but their desire to do something unique meant they were always ahead of the pack. Throughout, Netflix was completely committed to two mutually supportive ideas: be unique and stay focused.

To digress (again), I remain fascinated by the clash of two incredibly focused and well-managed brands, Netflix and Disney. I happen to be a huge fan of both their CEOs, and currently these companies are on a path of mutual destruction, or so we're told. I would argue that those who think Disney+ will fail in their attack on Netflix, or think Netflix is in big trouble because of Disney+, simply don't understand strategy. While I know Netflix would use different words to describe what they are, the Netflix difference is that they are essentially our streaming content library. Disney's point of difference is the creation of family entertainment, and they are simply deciding to more fully capture the total value of that content. There is a human limit to total screen time, so they will surely hurt each other, but Disney won't kill Netflix, and Netflix won't kill Disney. I'd be much more concerned about collateral damage to everyone else who competes for our screen time, because make no mistake, both of these companies will succeed.

As 2020 began, Disney+ was said to be worth $108 billion on its own, or 69 percent of the total value of Netflix. After just six weeks, it was worth more than ViacomCBS, Discovery, AMC, Lionsgate, Twitter, Snap, and Roku—combined. While I certainly don't know exactly how this will shake out, if you're not Disney or Netflix, the kitchen just got really hot.

Bob Iger is a CEO superhero because he made three incredibly smart, focused, and brave acquisitions and because he had the strategic courage to claim a larger share of the spoils created by the excellence of the content his company creates. Let's pause to note that when he made the decision to create Disney+, he made it with the understanding that this decision would cost a few billion a year for several years out. Make that four incredibly smart, brave, big decisions—all driven by a clear, long-term vision. Retailers of Disney merchandise had better keep their heads up, as they may just be next in line to feel the impact of his desire to realize more of the value chain created by Disney content. Reed Hastings is a CEO superhero because he clearly has seen this possibility coming for years, and he has spent billions to build the quantity and quality of his content library, to the point that we would find it hard to live without it. Strategically, I think both of these guys can see around corners.

Wait. Hold the presses. While we all sit at home watching Netflix, COVID-19 has shuttered Disney's Parks and Cruises business, not to mention cinemas and much of the sports business that supports ESPN. Iger, in the process of making his way gracefully out the door, was just yanked back into a burning building. This man has controlled all the variables. He's pulled all the right levers. And now he's hit by a global pandemic? We can assume that the minute he realized the broadly destructive implications of this virus, he poured himself a very stiff drink. We can also assume that, post-cocktail, he started working on Disney's COVID-recovery strategy.

This virus sucks. It kills human beings. It kills businesses owned and run by human beings. It is an uncontrollable variable. Really well-run companies in a virus-decimated industry have suffered greatly, while poorly run companies in more "virus-friendly" industries have prospered. As it turns out, the universe is random. Of these two incredibly well-run companies, Netflix was simply better positioned for a world that is sheltering in place. Disney was less fortunate, and their recovery will be much tougher, but for the record, my money is still on both of them to prosper.

In the mid-1990s I was running an ad agency in Seattle, and we had created what we billed as the first agency-based digital studio. A guy named **Jeff Bezos** rang and asked if we could help him improve a website. He wanted to sell books online. Their "office" was a few blocks away from ours, in an abandoned warehouse where the Amazon team (all eight of them) had taken the doors off their hinges to use as desks. They were incredibly proud of the fact that they had about a hundred books in that warehouse, waiting to be mailed out. I was too dumb to realize they were about to change the world, and instead of begging for a job I evaluated the business opportunity.

The point is, succeed or fail, Jeff Bezos was committed to doing something completely unique. I don't know how far down the road he could see at that time, but it doesn't really matter. Whatever you may think about Amazon, it's a uniquely amazing accomplishment, and I guess we can all agree that Jeff Bezos pretty much succeeded. We now have Echo to translate our every wish into an order that's delivered within a day or two, so anything that's not a deeply considered purchase decision can go directly from thought to delivery with zero friction along the way. Amazon's version of Disney+ is to fully capture the delivery value by creating or acquiring a delivery company. Better keep those stock prices up if you're FedEx, UPS, or DHL. Or maybe we should ask Mr. Bezos to privatize and fix USPS for us?

Now let's look at the opposite end of the spectrum for a useful cautionary tale. Founded in 2010 by **Adam Neumann**, WeWork was positioned as a trailblazing technology pioneer. Neumann talked about his company—once reported to be valued around $60 billion—in world-changing terms. But there were a couple issues on the table. First, WeWork wasn't really a pioneer; workspace sharing had been around for years. Second, it wasn't actually a technology company; it was a real estate play. It used technology, but so does everyone and everything.

I'm including this story to illustrate an important point: You can't make difference up. You can't pretend you're something you're not, no matter how much you spend on PR. As someone once said, "You can only sell sizzle for so long; sooner or later you have to sit down and eat." Sadly, you can sell sizzle for long enough to walk away with a lot of other people's money. Neumann may have actually believed his own bullshit, but at heart he was a good old-fashioned con man. Given the scale of the con, and the shady financial manipulation conducted behind the scenes, he should have walked away humbled and broke, but that's just not the world we live in. Placed in other cultural contexts, people go to jail for less, but again, that's not the world we live in. Thankfully, the con was discovered before an IPO happened and innocent investors were fleeced. Realistically, the value of WeWork's contribution to the world parallels Neumann's moral value—something between not much and nothing.

Adam Neumann is different, but not in a way that is true. Not in a way that creates advantage. Not in a way that is compelling. Unfortunately, like his company, he made himself into a fictional character.

These are just a few of the most recognizable names from the land of startups. I could add more stories, but the key plot points become repetitive. Instead, here's a highly subjective list of startups that created something entirely different. Because that difference held relevance to a lot of people, the company succeeded and, in succeeding, it changed the world:

- Yvon Chouinard founded Patagonia and should be your hero for a number of reasons.
- Sam Walton founded Walmart.
- Fred Smith founded FedEx.
- Larry Ellison founded Oracle.
- Marc Benioff founded Salesforce.
- Richard Branson founded Virgin.
- Sergey Brin and Larry Page founded Google.
- Mark Zuckerberg founded Facebook.
- Chad Hurley, Steve Chen, and Jawed Karim founded YouTube.
- Elon Musk founded PayPal and then Tesla.
- Brian Chesky, Joe Gebbia, and Nathan Blecharczyk founded Airbnb.
- Pierre Omidyar founded eBay.
- Jack Dorsey, Noah Glass, Biz Stone, and Evan Williams founded Twitter.

We don't have to like these people or the companies they founded, but we have to recognize that they had an impact on our world, even if we never used their services. Like pioneers do, many took advantage of a new frontier. They saw opportunity where others did not.

In them we see the qualities we must develop in ourselves if we're going to do different.

We will always need people like this, especially on today's frontiers of health sciences, food supply, and the environment. Innovation in health sciences will see us living longer lives, adding to the stress on a planet that soon may not be able to support all of us. Innovative new food sources are a key counterbalance, as well as a necessity if we are to solve for global warming. Cleaner energy innovations are essential to addressing this global warming challenge. Yes, folks, it's all very real, so where are the startups that will find ways to fix this mess? Can this be the next frontier for those who think and act different, please?

WAIT A MINUTE, WHY ARE ALL THESE STARTUP FOLK HEROES MEN?

Forgive me in advance for wandering off topic, but I want to take a moment to consider something important here. I promise it'll lead us back to difference, but it might take a few pages.

Looking at this startup hall of fame, I realized this is just a long list of—guys. Where are the examples of women who have embraced doing things differently? Women who have built companies that have changed our world? This is a tough—and anxiety-producing—question to try to answer.

Let's start by agreeing that, in business, the odds have been stacked against women forever. This has nothing to do with women's acumen, of course, and everything to do with old power structures reasserting themselves over and over again. Not that long ago, women were actively excluded from business leadership, and today women remain tragically underrepresented. I could trot out countless statistics and case studies to support this claim, but instead I'll use the following statistic from Clear Company as a representative fact: in 2019, there were fewer women CEOs than there were male CEOs named David. Perhaps the scariest thing about this little factoid is that I actually believe it.

Yes, things are getting better for women, but not remotely fast enough.

That said, when I realized my stories of world-changing success through difference featured only men, I suspected the fault lay with me. I'm older. I'm male. I must be biased. So I read up on successful women entrepreneurs. The good news: there is an increasing number. The bad news: when I applied the filters of "difference" and "scale" to this list, few names remained.

Again, this is where I'm probably talking myself into trouble, but away I go. I'm a strategist, and I felt there had to be a pattern that would help me understand this. My working assumption became that we are moving through stages. In today's somewhat more enlightened culture, an increasing number of women are bucking the odds and creating highly successful businesses, but not "zero to one" businesses, at scale, yet.

Is timing the issue? Have women simply not had enough time in power positions to create these kinds of earthshaking business disruptions? For obvious reasons, women may be more focused on simply succeeding in a male-dominated business culture than they are on creating something completely different. We also know that women are not remotely as well supported as their male counterparts when it comes to VC funding, which has supported most of the world-changing ideas mentioned previously.

All of this is by way of apology. I've been blithely writing about a bunch of men who have built truly different, game-changing businesses, and I'm still not totally sure why there hasn't been a woman in sight yet. So I started asking women about difference. Somewhat to my surprise, not to mention relief, none told me I was speaking nonsense, not even my wife. Names of undeniably powerful, successful, recognizable businesswomen were raised, then eliminated when we applied the filter of difference at scale. Except one: Oprah.

Oprah Winfrey can rightfully claim to have created something meaningfully unique. Without question, Winfrey has walked a different path, inspiring millions of people in a way that had never been done before. Though the business Oprah created may not look so unique on the surface, she is most definitely one of a kind. Not to mention the fact that she has succeeded wildly within a business model that had traditionally been run as a boys' club.

In 2011, as Oprah's television show was winding up its final season, reporter Emily Sohn wrote:

> [Oprah] also broke down the traditional barriers of journalism. She transformed the book-publishing industry. She made the very private very public. And she prepared a mass audience to celebrate differences among people, regardless of color, disabilities, or sexual orientation.[2]

In the same article, Sohn quoted Mary McNamara, a television critic with the *Los Angeles Times*, who said, "I cannot overstate the impact that she has had on our culture. You see it everywhere, from the explosion of memoirs to social media to journalists sharing their own opinions and own stories. That all started with Oprah. She changed the nature of journalism."[3]

Clearly Oprah belongs on the list (not that she cares). A few other important names kept popping up in my search:

- Entertainers such as **Beyoncé**. Brilliantly and uniquely talented people, but women who are succeeding within—as opposed to fundamentally changing—an established business model.
- Women who are incredibly talented but have succeeded in established paradigms. **Indra Nooyi** at Pepsico, **Susan Wojcicki** at Google and now YouTube, **Sheryl Sandberg** at Facebook, **Wang Laichun** at Luxshare,

2.   Emily Sohn, "How Oprah Winfrey Changed America," May 25, 2011, NBC News.

3.   Sohn, "How Oprah Winfrey Changed America."

> **Denise Coates** at Bet365, **Debbie Fields** and her namesake cookies, and fashion designer **Tory Burch**.
> - **Cher Wang** has been massively successful in creating and running HTC, but this is not a business that's founded on true difference.

Arguably, **Sara Blakely** has done something more truly different through her invention of Spanx—an old idea beautifully brought forward in time, through a unique brand attitude.

There's also **Katrina Lake** of Stitch Fix fame. Keep in mind, when she took Stitch Fix public in November 2017, it was the first female-led IPO in over a year. This company has been profitable since 2014 and created $1.2 billion in revenue in its fiscal 2018. Selling personalized wardrobing and simplifying a very complex decision, they now boast more than 3.2 million clients. Maybe they're not changing our world, but both Spanx and Stitch Fix feel pretty unique to me, and I would hope to find them on the next list I see.

My search also turned up an interesting piece in *The New York Times* about **Lynn Jurich**, founder and CEO of Sunrun, the leading US installer of residential solar. First, let me admit that I'd never heard of her, which may simply be my own ignorance, but may also be attributable to the fact that women leaders receive significantly less press attention than their male counterparts (just ask Senator Elizabeth Warren). It wasn't only Jurich's obvious success that struck me, it was her humble response to that success: "One hundred percent of people said it wouldn't work and gave me this dismissive message. 'Well, there's a lot of sophisticated people working on that stuff. Go home, little girl.'"[4] She didn't give up, and as of 2021, her company has over 550,000 customers and reported a

---

4. David Gelles, "She's Taking on Elon Musk on Solar. And Winning." *The New York Times,* Jan 23, 2020.

net earnings of $4.2 billion.[5] Here's an intriguing mantra that represents her daily morning meditation: "All people and all circumstances are my allies."[6] *The Times* article makes it clear that Lynn Jurich has a unique and trusting management style. While she is kicking Elon Musk's ass in solar, she still sees him as an ally, as per her daily meditation.

While the number of women who have created zero-to-one businesses at scale is abysmally low (at least so far), I suspect the number of women who have changed the way business happens within companies—like many of the leaders named above—is much higher than we realize.

As a token of equal acceptance or, more accurately, Pyrrhic victory, I must mention **Elizabeth Holmes** of Theranos. This would have been an incredible case study in the creation of differentiated advantage—if only it had been real. It wasn't, and Elizabeth Holmes should find time for an expensive dinner, paid for by Adam Neumann's loot, where they can both toast what might have been if they'd only told the truth.

Success is success, and the women named here are wildly accomplished. However, if we're looking for examples of culture-changing, at-scale, embedded-difference businesses (and in this case we are), unfortunately (as of this writing) it's still a man's world.

As a somewhat encouraging point of reference, 2019 saw more woman-led businesses funded by VCs than ever before. But consider that just 2.5 percent of all venture-capital-backed startups have an all-female founding team. Only 9 percent of the venture capitalists investing in tech startups are women. And even in 2019, only slightly more than one-fifth of all-American VC investment went to startups where at least one of the founders is a woman.

---

5.   Sunrun, Investor Relations (website), accessed July 21, 2020, https://investors.sunrun.com/.
6.   David Gelles, "She's Taking on Elon Musk on Solar. And Winning." *The New York Times*, Jan 23, 2020.

Clearly some deep cultural forces are at work here. Forces that need to change. By this time, doesn't everyone believe that the world would be a better place if more of our nations were run by women? German chancellor Angela Merkel has been amazing. In New Zealand, Prime Minister Jacinda Ardern is offering us a master course in empathetic, highly effective leadership. Any chance of making her an offer to change "companies"?

Surely things have to get better, and I can't wait to see the list of truly new ideas that will be led by women. I hope, at least, we're through the phase where women felt they had to act like men in order to succeed. Given the way men have pretty much screwed this planet over, emulating the male of the species seems like a really bad idea.

In writing this, I have felt like a very awkward skater on really thin ice. Not trusting my own thoughts on this topic, I had a fascinating, wide-ranging conversation with Lisa Hetfield, interim director of the Institute for Women's Leadership at Rutgers. Thankfully, Lisa didn't laugh at me or say something along the lines of "You poor, misguided man." Among the many challenges women face in business, she talked about the difficulty of being the "only." Women in leadership positions can suffer from a profound sense of isolation, a lack of true peers with whom to share experiences. That old adage "It's lonely at the top" rings especially true for women in leadership. Being different can be rough going at times.

DIVERSITY BREEDS DIFFERENCE.

All of this talk about the difficulty faced by women in business leads us to the more general topic of diversity. (Yep, we're sticking with this tangent a bit longer.) Sadly, you see the same patterns with African American and Latinx businesspeople. Turns out, if you want to change the world with a new and different idea, it helps to be white and male.

This is not an unfamiliar story. If our world had been operating the way it should, about half of all completely unique, world-changing ideas would have come from women and about 30 percent from the black and Hispanic population, half of whom are male and not yet accounted for. Very roughly, about 65 percent in total. But institutional bias has worked hard against these developments, and the results are pretty damning. In fact, even if we shift the filter from completely unique ideas to plain old business leadership, we find a *Fortune* study that looked at sixteen leading companies with a combined population of eight hundred thousand. In 2017, a fairly astounding 72 percent of their senior managers were white men.

Let me repeat. White males are a bit less than 30 percent of the general population, yet they occupy 72 percent of our senior management positions. Interestingly, as I repeat this statistic to friends, no one is shocked. The somewhat common response is "Yeah, seems shocking when you look at the number, but it's not really that surprising."

Returning to the subject of this book, let's consider this: I think it's a pretty solid hypothesis to say that diversity is a breeding ground for difference. If you put ten smart, imaginative white men from similar family and academic backgrounds in a room together, you've created a lot of groupthink. Sure, maybe they'll have fun. Maybe they can tell stories everyone in the room will relate to, but there's a lot of idea redundancy built into that room. Instead, if you put ten smart, imaginative people from wildly different backgrounds into that room, you've just created a much more interesting mélange. There will be less agreement, less verbal shorthand, more debate, and—most importantly—more difference.

Malcolm Forbes put it this way: "Diversity is the art of thinking independently—together."

Difference comes from difference. Diversity creates difference. Homogeneity works against difference. Of course, this hypothesis doesn't just apply to doing different. It could just as easily apply to making better decisions in general. To that end, we all benefit from hiring for diversity. We may even have to change our practices to do so. Note: I do not mean lower our standards; I mean change them and drop our presumptions about who can meet them. Be demanding, but not in a rigid, old-school way that creates homogeneity. Be demanding in a way that creates diversity of background, which surely will lead to diversity of thought.

Hire diversity, then make an effort to create and curate diverse, multidisciplinary groups. Then—this next point is absolutely critical—actively encourage debate. Position debate as an essential precursor to truly great ideas. Make sure the resulting increase in debate is always centered around the ideas rather than the people. Do this, then watch as your company becomes more unique, more innovative, more responsive, more successful.

Isn't it worth a shot?

While it seems intuitive that a more diverse team will create better outcomes on a number of fronts, I had a hard time finding "proof" of this hypothesis. If we briefly use "innovation" as a proxy for "difference," things get interesting. Consider a "diversity and innovation" study done in 2018 by Boston Consulting Group. The most interesting result BCG found was a strong and statistically significant correlation between the diversity of management teams and overall innovation. Companies that reported above-average diversity on their management teams also reported innovation revenue that was 19 percentage points higher than that of companies with below-average leadership diversity—it accounted for 45 percent of total revenue versus just 26 percent. For large companies desperate to become more innovative, this is a huge advantage.

McKinsey—always a good name to mention when looking at business trends—did an interesting study in 2008–2010. They looked at the executive board composition of a large number of companies in France, Germany, the United Kingdom, and the United States. The available information dictated that "diversity" be defined by the presence of women and questionably titled "foreign nationals," but let's just go with that for now. Over the three years measured, companies in the top quartile of board diversity experienced a 53 percent higher return on equity and a 14 percent higher EBIT than those in the bottom quartile. Sure, you can poke holes in this and argue causality. For example, is it the case that more successful companies are inherently more enlightened, so also tend to have more diverse boards? We can't know for sure. So for now, let's just accept this as a data point to consider.

One prominent company in that top quartile was Adidas, which sees diversity as a strategic goal. Through setting goals and measuring their progress, Adidas now has 33 percent of its leadership positions occupied by women. It's not 50 percent, and the fact that this has to be a long-term strategic goal in the first place is surely saddening, but it's a hell of a lot better than most large companies. Pre-pandemic, I was flying Emirates and watched a very serious ad for Standard Chartered, claiming that only 15 percent of all finance jobs are filled by women. They state, somewhat vaguely, that they have set an ambitious "goal" of 30 percent. Again, points for making the effort, but how sad is it that even 30 percent seems like a vaguely defined and distant goal?

Diversity has become too much like a box to be ticked. A duty or obligation. A way to keep the critics at bay. Something to be fixed. Overall, a reactive and defensive strategy. I would like to see diversity repositioned as a proactive and offensive strategy. Diversity is not a fix; it's an opportunity. It's a source of competitive advantage. It can help you win.

Don't embrace diversity out of obligation. Embrace diversity to win.

Diversity of thought will come with diversity of people, but only if it is also actively encouraged and cultivated. As an example, my company creates positioning strategies for our clients. For every strategy I create, the more my partner challenges my thinking, the better that strategy becomes. While I have to admit that I hate being wrong, I hate being bad much, much more. In writing this book, I can say that every single criticism of my thinking has made it better. Even when I didn't agree with a criticism, the thinking it inspired made my point stronger and clearer.

One sure sign of a healthy, successful organization is the active presence of debate. If your people can't call bullshit on leadership thinking, you're doomed to a mundane existence of strategic short-sightedness. Pursuing internal criticism will definitely be frustrating at times but, trust me, it'll be worth it.

When I was running an advertising agency, I organized a weekly meeting with a young group of our best and brightest—smart and generally skeptical people who, I hoped, would yield a unique and challenging perspective. One of my personal favorites in the group really disappointed me in the first couple of meetings, as he barely spoke. When I asked him if he agreed with everything I said and did, he replied, "Of course not, but I don't want to embarrass you in front of the group." But that was the whole purpose of the meetings. When I told him it was actually selfish and unfair for him to hold back, he got it. Over time, he offered up some blistering criticism, but it was a perspective that made me a much better leader, and our company became much more successful as a result.

Netflix has essentially institutionalized this idea with a "radically honest" approach to feedback—up and down their organization. If someone is acting poorly, or thinking about doing something dumb, they will quickly hear about it from those around them. Institutionalizing this idea, over time, has served to take most (but not all) of the sting out of it, and it is just a really smart, productive way for people to work.

One last personal story before we move on. When running an ad agency in Chicago, I visited an organization called Off The Street Club, in West Garfield Park, considered one of the most dangerous neighborhoods in the country. The club offers neighborhood kids a safe place to go for "games, play, and mentorship." Local ad agencies partnered with the organization for a program offering opportunities for kids to gain work experience in agency "mail rooms." Ralph Campagna, the club's amazing leader, took a group of us on a tour that day, and I'll never forget something he said. Standing at the front door, pointing at the shining skyscrapers in the distance, he told us, "To these kids, those buildings might as well be another planet." That planet was filled with white, confident, busy people who spoke a completely foreign tongue. In that moment, I realized that the main benefit of working in a mail room at an ad agency wasn't the actual work experience; it was seeing that the people in those impressive buildings weren't any smarter than the kids in West Garfield Park. The people in those buildings said stupid things, did stupid things, and probably wouldn't have survived a day if forced to walk in those kids' shoes. The point was for those kids to see they were just as smart and capable as the inhabitants of that other planet, just in a different way. The point was for us to learn from each other.

I'll move on from this topic now and leave the larger, more complex arguments for diversity to the experts. I'm simply adding "the creation of difference" to the myriad of reasons you should build organizational diversity. In all its forms, diversity is a powerful, but too often untapped, source of competitive advantage.

Okay, tangent over. I started this talking about massive, world-changing, ground-up difference. Let's move on to discussing two other kinds of difference: uncovering difference from within and the creation of a different point of view.

UNCOVERING DIFFERENCE WHEN IT'S SOMEONE ELSE'S PLANE AND IT'S ALREADY IN THE AIR.

We've just talked about a lot of famous people who built something world changing and unique from the ground up. But there are other difference heroes in the business world: those who take something seemingly ordinary and make it unique. These folks are not generally famous, because they work from within a company. They don't create something new, but they do have a vision. They also have the difficult task of convincing an entire organization to follow that vision into the land of difference, to zig when everyone else is zagging. Keep in mind that, by definition, the organizations they work for have been zagging for years, along with everyone else in their category. We've already discussed institutional bias against difference. As they say, the only person who likes change is a wet baby. These visionary marketers must not only create a radically new way of looking at an old problem, but also promote difference such that reluctant decision makers within the organization will get on board.

When we go into, or look inside, the organizations in which these shifts happen, we often find crisis. Not surprisingly, crisis promotes change. With very few exceptions, people call consultants like me only when things aren't going so well. As an insightful client in need of a brand turnaround said recently: "Let's not waste the opportunity inherent to a good crisis."

So what does it take to uncover true difference within an existing brand and business? This is essentially an act of ruthless excavation. You'll need to look at the company with clear eyes, identify the differences, and be ruthlessly honest in assessing how compelling those differences really are, how much competitive advantage they actually possess.

Michelangelo once suggested that sculpting was simple—you just look at the rock, see the beautiful shape that lies within, then chip away the bits you don't need. This is a great metaphor for the task at hand here. When uncovering difference, the answer is already in the room; you just need to see the beautiful shape inside all of that information.

This idea brings me to one of my bigger failures as a consultant. Several years ago, we worked with the Levi's for Women team to create a differentiated positioning strategy. For years they'd been losing market share to designer jeans. Some of the designer brands became quite big, but what really held the audience's attention was the rotating door of shiny objects—the constant churn of fashion brands. So Levi's jumped into that pool and created designer jeans of their own, hoping to sell them at Barney's for a couple of hundred bucks. Predictably, the jeans made it onto the shelf but never really made it off.

Why? Because Levi's were not being true to their brand. Levi Strauss stands for high-quality, reliable, resilient, authentic jeans. Levi's are strong of character. Particularly versus many of these fragile designer brands, Levi's were also, literally, physically stronger. We argued that this was the positioning opportunity. We believed that, for women, "in strength there is beauty." No apologies. No pretension. Like the women who wear them, Levi's are strong, and therefore beautiful. Of course, I thought it was a masterful positioning strategy, completely true to the brand it served. But, for a bunch of organizational reasons, this positioning idea never took root, and Levi's continued to chase a market that could never be theirs. Maybe today, with more-savvy marketers in charge and Levi's enjoying a bit of a renaissance, it's not too late?

A couple of iconic car brands, VW and MINI, found their difference within themselves. In both cases, they very effectively took a unique, brutally honest (not to mention creative and fun) approach to who they were in the mind of the marketplace. Microsoft is under great management these days, and I'd love to see their marketers uncover and shine the brand that lies within. It's there, lying in wait—just chip the stone away. When challenged years ago by Reebok, Nike forgot who they were for a short period and reacted to something that was essentially a fashion trend. Nike is not a fashion brand, and once they realized that their superpower is competitive performance, they crushed the challenge. Something to remember, as Adidas has mounted a serious fashion challenge of late.

A very smart marketer named Jostein Solheim once ran Ben & Jerry's, which had been acquired a decade earlier by Unilever. At one point Jostein described his role as "re-radicalizing" Ben & Jerry's—a description I think the two iconic founders would have loved. He intuitively understood that doing things differently was in the DNA of this truly unique brand, and he made a conscious effort to show his organization how much he valued it, which was exactly what that organization needed to see. One memorable story involved a seasonal promotion recommended by his marketing team, involving a flavor named "Schweddy Balls," based on an Alec Baldwin *SNL* skit. Whatever his personal perspective was, by approving this, Jostein confirmed he "got it." It's probably worth mentioning that they sold out of that flavor, and the press they received boosted sales across the entire brand. Jostein knew that what you actually do is much more important than what you might say. He also knew that brands are built from the inside out.

It's one thing to find meaningful difference within a brand or business; it's another thing entirely to take action based on what you find—to *do* different. Not all companies are actually in touch with their difference, and a much smaller subset are culturally prepared to promote that difference in the world in which they operate.

FIND A DIFFERENT POINT OF VIEW.

Then again, not all companies can find difference within. What happens then? What if the sculptor can't find a beautiful shape in the rock? This is the toughest scenario for the marketer, but perhaps the most personally rewarding if you can figure out the puzzle. When the marketer gets this right, it's like an act of magic. Yes, there was probably lots of analysis involved, but in these cases the marketer used that analysis to fuel a long and intuitively powered leap of the imagination.

If your business or brand doesn't offer any real difference in the user experience, you need to find a differentiating point of view. It's an act of creation, but where do you find your inspiration? Although the insight that leads to a differentiating point of view can come from anywhere, it generally comes from the way your audience views your category or brand. Strategy is essentially pattern recognition, and that's what you need to do: scan cultural category dynamics, looking for one of those patterns.

Also consider Newton's third law: For every action there is an equal and opposite reaction. Look for marketplace forces or trends that are working to the detriment of your audience and ask yourself if you can create an equal and opposite reaction. Although you need to be wary of borrowing interest from an idea that doesn't really connect to your brand, this can be an interesting path to positioning opportunities that are both differentiating and "culturally noisy"—ideas that will create a disruption in the force, ideas that will be talked about. We'll discuss all of this in more detail later. For now, let me take you behind the scenes to show you how this works.

I've already mentioned Dove, where there was no real difference available. Working with the Unilever brand team, our strategy group conducted consumer research and essentially created a differentiating point of view around the idea that beauty comes from within. Because that point of view was strong and ran so counter to category norms, it was culturally noisy, meaning it provoked thought and discussion. But how did we get there?

The Dove brand team, led by a woman named Silvia Lagnado, was facing a reluctant, all-male leadership team. Knowing that their perspective, grounded in category convention, might be an obstacle, the brand team polled the leadership team's wives and daughters prior to the meeting. When making their recommendations, the brand team very effectively, not to mention bravely, brought these voices into the room. They sold the strategy, and paired with the uniquely compelling "Real Beauty" marketing communications campaign, created primarily by Ogilvy & Mather to drive that cultural provocation home, they made history.

This is the profile of a difference-creator: relentless in the pursuit of a meaningfully disruptive idea; relentless in selling that idea to the organization within which it resides.

How about the people who buy into the idea? They need to be ready to leap too. When we went to work with MSNBC, they were a small, culturally quiet, middle-of-the-road cable news channel. It was, until recently, led by Phil Griffin. While I do love to boast about how smart some of our strategies are, this one kind of wrote itself. We had Fox News on the right and CNN in the middle. The left was wide open, and MSNBC was already leaning that way a bit with Keith Olbermann. To cut a much longer story short, when we asked Phil, and MSNBC's super-smart CMO, Sharon Otterman, if they were willing to embrace a strong brand position on the left, the answer was an enthusiastic yes.

Again, this story is not about the intelligence or creativity of the differentiating position we created, it's about the bravery and commitment of people like Phil and Sharon. Bit by bit, they placed the bricks in the wall. Keith gave way to Rachel Maddow, who was joined by a prime time cast of liberal commentators as MSNBC became "passionately progressive." Lately, MSNBC has occasionally enjoyed a Nielsen ratings lead among cable news channels— something we could only have dreamed of as we put the strategy together. At that time, NBC was owned by GE, led by Jeff Immelt, whose politics were very conservative. Whenever an MSNBC commentator said something particularly offensive to Mr. Immelt (pretty much every night), Phil knew he'd get an earful from his bosses. But he persevered. He stayed the course.

How about Corona beer? Several years ago, the beer marketplace was dominated by loud, high-energy advertising populated mainly by beautiful women, all clearly communicating that the world of beer was a young man's playground. But, as we did with Dove, someone said, "They're all zigging; let's zag." Corona hit the beach and replaced loud words and music with quiet waves. Implicitly, and very confidently, they told everyone to chill out. It was completely different in a way we all found compelling, whether we liked the beer or not. It was quiet in execution, but culturally it was very noisy.

Or Axe. Working within Unilever, a bunch of young guys with high testosterone levels created a personal-care brand for young men, entirely around the idea that boys are trying to attract girls. Not exactly a huge insight, but taken to an extreme it became a highly differentiating point of view to build a brand position on. The Axe team and their advertising agency partners essentially took this idea for a run all the way to its outer limits. There was nothing special about the product; they just made the idea as different and compelling to their audience as possible. It was ridiculously successful, and both Unilever and that group of brand people deserve huge kudos for essentially creating difference out of nothing.

Whether you're building something entirely new, uncovering compelling difference within a brand, or leveraging a radically different point of view, pushing for difference takes vision, drive, and a heavy dose of risk tolerance. In other words, to bring back my newly coined idea: it requires high DQ.

So now I'm back to that nagging question: If we know difference can lead to mind-blowing successes, why do we hesitate to do different? Why do we revere our difference heroes but shy away from walking our own truly different paths? Why is high DQ so rare?

It won't surprise you to hear I have some opinions about that.

"Always remember that you are absolutely unique. Just like everyone else."

—Margaret Mead

PART II

DIFFERENCE DAMPENERS

Not like Homer would I write,
Not like Dante if I might,
Not like Shakespeare at his best,
Not like Goethe or the rest,
Like myself, however small,
Like myself, or not at all.

—William Allingham, "Blackberries"

CHAPTER 4

OUR PARENTS AND OUR INSTITUTIONS

"Be weird. Be random. Be who you are. Because you never know who would love the person you hide."

—C. S. Lewis

Let's hypothesize for a moment. Let's say that, in addition to characteristics such as IQ and EQ, we're all born with something called DQ. Then life happens, molding our DQ, lifting it or dampening it. Some of us have such a high inherent DQ that, despite the dampening forces in our lives, we continue to chart our own course. Others—perhaps the majority of people—cave to the difference-dampening forces at an early age and stick to the prescribed path.

Okay, now let's dream a bit. Imagine a world in which parents celebrate their children's DQ. Visualize schools and churches that understand the cultural value of DQ and actively cultivate it. Add in companies that see the business-building power of DQ and promote it. How would a difference-enhancing environment like this change the life you're living?

Now hold on to that dream while we look at what's actually happening in our world: we are socialized to associate "difference" with "risk," to our collective detriment. Where does this come from? In the coming chapters, we'll discuss three common difference-dampening forces: our parents and institutions, our companies, and ourselves.

TO LOVE AND PROTECT, BUT AT WHAT COST?

"You are a marvel. You are unique. In all the years that have passed, there has never been another child like you. Your legs, your arms, your clever fingers, the way you move. You may become a Shakespeare, a Michelangelo, a Beethoven. You have the capacity for anything."
—Pablo Casals

We'll begin with our parents. We love them, and they love us. Our parents want the best for us, but even more importantly, they want to keep us safe. In the minds of most parents, "best" and "safest" are not found in difference. For the vast majority of parents, "best" and "safest" mean camouflaging your difference in the cloak of the mainstream. From an evolutionary perspective, this makes sense. Our parents' prime directive is to nudge us into the center of the herd. Who can blame them? Those who stand out risk being eaten by whatever predator lurks behind those eyes glowing in the dark. While the stakes of today's parenting game are not usually as dramatic as this, it can feel like they are.

Growing up is tough enough for kids who fit in; for outliers it's a jungle of ridicule and rejection. Sure, great teachers can make a huge difference in the lives of kids with high DQ, and these days outliers can connect with people like themselves on the internet, which can help a lot. Still, high-DQ kids usually have a tough road ahead. Unfortunately, many parents try to file down their kids' rough edges in a misguided attempt to smooth that road.

While some of us have been blessed with parents who have celebrated and defended our DQ, in most cases, if a teacher told a parent, "Your child is really different," that parent would automatically wonder what's wrong.

When exploring the forces that might act to dampen a child's DQ, I found that the most critical developmental age seems to be nine through eleven, when kids really start to notice and assign importance to conformity. Research shows that physically attractive and socially comfortable kids fit in better than others. Also, some literature suggests a pass-on effect—parents who didn't fit in often raise children who don't fit in. No real surprises there.

But this did surprise me: the vast majority of the writing on children and difference presumes that parents place high value on their kids' ability to fit in. In other words, the starting assumption is that the objective is to blend in, not stand out. Much less common is literature about helping children embrace and navigate their uniqueness.

Therapist Dana Belletiere offers an uncommonly encouraging take on kids with high DQ:

> Given support and encouragement, an awkward teenager that doesn't fit in can grow into a confident and unique adult with something brand new to create or share or teach. This is a gift to the world, should we choose to recognize it as such—a chance to grow and to expand and to learn, and maybe experience something beautiful. There are so many thousands of one-note voices out there singing. What a relief it is to hear original song!

The world needs more therapists—and parents—like Dana Belletiere.

In Australia, where I worked for several years, I learned about a cultural phenomenon they call the tall poppy syndrome: if a poppy grows tall enough to stand out from the field, it needs to be cut down. While people see America as a land of opportunity, which in many ways it is, we have our own version of this syndrome. We celebrate those who play the same game as everyone else and win. But we reject those who play their own game. Here, being the tallest poppy is just fine. Being a red flower in a sea of green plants? Not so much.

In this world of "better, not different," we encourage our kids to be smarter. A high IQ is seen as a positive characteristic. More and more, parents are paying attention to the development of children's EQ, also seen as a positive characteristic. In today's world, the more IQ and EQ you have, the better—or so we believe. How about DQ?

Later in life, these kids will apply for jobs in companies that filter prospects based on some interpretation of IQ and EQ. How many even consider DQ? I wish they would. Anyone interested in developing a DQ test?

Those entrepreneurs we discussed earlier—I'm pretty confident all of them stood out as kids. I'm willing to bet they were generally viewed as "different." Did their parents encourage their difference? Did they fight it? How many sleepless nights did they spend worrying about their different kids? At what point did they accept that their kids would always be square pegs in a world of round holes? Did these future entrepreneurs thrive because their parents nurtured their DQ, or because they had such high DQ they didn't care what anyone else thought about them?

We know a young Steve Jobs was called different, and not in a positive way, on many occasions. Without his business success, would he have been just another guy in need of a shower and a pair of shoes?

Growing up, I think most of us have either witnessed or personally experienced the active, and sometimes hostile, rejection of difference by the mainstream. Particularly for parents, at a time when they're looking for the safest and most certain path for their children, encouraging difference remains a high-risk approach. But what damage do we do by forcing unique kids to hide who they really are? What's left when we squeeze all their difference out?

I wish I had some brilliant advice for parents. Our instinct to keep our kids from harm will always come first, and unfortunately, standing out as different invites harm. At this point in time, this dynamic just doesn't feel very malleable to me. So we have to find some way to change the world around our kids with high DQ. We need to break up the herd mentality by highlighting the successes of those who followed a different path. We need to celebrate those who would not, not even under duress, give up their world-changing visions. We need to help kids with high DQ develop the confidence to stand strong in a world that fears difference. Being different takes a lot of courage, and parenting difference might take even more.

> "Do the other kids make fun of you? For how you talk?"
> "Sometimes."
> "So why don't you do something about it?
> You could learn to talk differently, you know."
> "But this is my voice. How would you be
> able to tell when I was talking?"
> —Lauren Oliver, *Before I Fall*

TEACHING CONFORMITY

Parents conspire against difference partly because they have experienced our institutions themselves. They know firsthand how tough it is to be unique. They know being different can feel like looking in the window from the cold, lonely outside. This is not what they want for their children.

Educational and religious institutions, for practical reasons, are heavily rules based. Their rule sets guide the thoughts, feelings, and behaviors of very large groups of people. As an inevitable extension, those who don't follow the rules must be dealt with, in ways both small and life changing. The paths are clear:

Follow the rules → stay out of trouble → fit in → good child.

Don't follow the rules → get in trouble → stand out → bad child.

In education this is an understandable response to a capacity-challenged system. Most schools, with their overworked and under-paid teachers, just don't have the bandwidth to deal with difference, so the system tries to minimize it. The default response to a child's difference is to "fix" it. Yes, some schools and individual teachers celebrate difference. But they remain the exception rather than the rule.

As I researched this topic, I ran across Sir Ken Robinson, a fascinating educator with a driving belief that schools are essentially knocking creativity out of our kids. If you're interested, search him and find his very articulate, interesting—and much better thought-out—perspective, encapsulated here:

"Some of the most brilliant, creative people I know did not do well at school. Many of them didn't really discover what they could do—and who they really were—until they'd left school and recovered from their education."

In religious institutions we see even less tolerance for difference than we see in education. These institutions, serving masses of people around the globe, have created clear rule sets that generally do not change over time. As with schools, most traditional religions do not facilitate exceptions. This is not an attack on organized religion, simply a recognition that any institution with such scale and such a deeply rooted rule set will inevitably suppress individuality.

Importantly, this is just the institutional perspective. Within these institutions operates a social perspective. As the social center of gravity for kids, this is particularly true of education. On campus, kids who are different are shunned by their peers. Yes, social media allows different kids to discover others like them online. But social media has a shadow side, too: it reinforces the importance of popularity, and it very tangibly brings the discomforts of school social dynamics into the home. The internet is the easiest place in the world to reject or bully people—not just leave them by the side of the road, but ensure they know when and why they're being left behind.

Teachers and clergy play out their own social dynamics within these institutions, as well. Most got into their positions by following rules rather than by breaking them. As rule followers, they just don't know what to do with difference. Children who are different can make people around them, including teachers and clergy, uncomfortable. Further, teachers and clergy are tasked with maintaining the status quo. Those who are different inevitably challenge that status quo. They challenge rules and assumptions. In other words, to the people in charge, those who are different can be a complete pain in the ass.

In high school, I was a card-carrying member of the pain-in-the-ass club. In my English class, I frequently disagreed with my teacher's analysis of books. It's fair to say I was an obnoxious jerk. So we struck a deal. She would give me a passing grade, and I would stay away from class. At the time I thought I had made a brilliant move, but in reality, we were both idiots—me for giving up a piece of my education, and her for failing to do her job. The point is that people like me are difficult for people like her. I refused to fit in, and she simply didn't have the time or patience to cater to a student who was a bit off-center. (Maybe more than a bit.)

Institutions that play an integral part in our personal development are simply not equipped to handle difference. Add in the social dynamics between peers within these institutions, and you've got an awful lot of built-in pressure to conform. There's no simple solution here, as the institutions I'm talking about simply operate better on similarity and consistency than they do on difference.

These institutions and their members operate best at the "normal" setting, which makes sense. The normal curve is fat in the middle because that's where most people sit, and institutions are set up to serve most people. The problem comes when they are forced to deal with those of us who sit at the much smaller ends of the curve. Their default response is to actively push people and thinking toward that fat middle. It's self-serving and in many ways essential to their operation. Their business models have little tolerance for difference.

Alternative schools exist—schools better built to nurture difference—but generally speaking they're accessible only to people who can afford them, or if they are public schools the waiting list to get in is a mile long. My daughter teaches at one such school, Synergy, in San Francisco, where she and her colleagues work with kids "as they are" rather than trying to shape them into what they "should be." In the absence of a school like this, what can we do for kids with high DQ? We can advocate for the importance of difference, we can seek and support extracurricular activities that nurture DQ, and we can love. In the absence of institutional support, simply being surrounded by people who love and celebrate your difference can go a long, long way.

Particularly in education, the stakes are getting higher as our planet staggers forward. As I write this, COVID-19 is still raging around the globe, disrupting every layer of society. As scary as this virus is, it may be just a warning shot over the bow, with bigger problems on the horizon. We need solutions to those problems. Whatever those solutions may be, one thing is certain: they are not going to emerge from conformity. We need people who can combine deep knowledge with the ability to ignore what has been and to focus totally on what can be.

Increasingly, the world will need high-DQ solutions to high-impact problems.

> *"The surest way to corrupt a youth is to instruct*
> *him to hold in higher esteem those who think*
> *alike than those who think differently."*
>
> —Friedrich Nietzsche

CHAPTER 5

OUR COMPANIES

"Not all those who wander are lost."

—Gandalf

Considering the ways we are socialized toward sameness by our parents, schools, and religious institutions, it's no wonder true difference—the kind that can drive everything from life-changing innovations to culturally noisy marketing strategy—is so rare. People who are trained to fit in are going to have a hard time creating and promoting ideas that stand out, especially in businesses—particularly large companies—where corporate culture can exert such a strong difference-dampening force.

The Wall Street Journal used census information to calculate that 36.2 percent of us work in large companies (2,500+ employees), while 24.9 percent work in midsize companies (100–2,500), and 38.9 percent in small companies (fewer than 100). No matter our company's size or stage of development, we all struggle against difference-dampening forces within and around our organizations.

But it's large companies that struggle with difference most. In part, this is a simple function of scale, and no fault of their own.

Like educational and religious institutions, their sheer size means they become heavily dependent on rule sets. Those who fit into those rule sets move up; those who do not generally find somewhere else to work.

Large companies can be difference-killers.

This isn't just me being critical. There are a host of reasons why, even if a difference-pusher like me ran a large company, that company would still struggle with difference (actually, they'd struggle with a lot of other things as well). Still, I believe even the biggest companies are malleable. More malleable, at least, than our other cultural institutions. Large companies can be high-DQ companies, if they really want to be. If they see difference as essential to business. If they see competitive advantage in difference. Perhaps this chapter will help that happen in some way?

Make no mistake, it's really hard to do different when operating at scale. Really hard. To illustrate, let's take a quick look at three large-company characteristics that typically get in the way: performance metrics, analysis dependence, and business model myopia.

PERFORMANCE METRICS

A well-run large company has broken its strategy into the performance metrics it needs most to succeed, and then it rewards its employees for the successful pursuit of those metrics. In other words, paychecks are driven by a very linear set of performance metrics. In many ways, difference is therefore a nonlinear performance characteristic trying to survive in a completely linear performance environment. Most large companies do not reward difference in any organized way, shape, or form.

By way of example, we've seen that difference is a leading indicator of the health of your brand. We've also seen that difference can be quantified and tracked. So, how many business leaders are assessed based on their brand's differentiation score? While I don't know the answer, I do know the number is low. This is an absolutely crazy state of affairs. Brand difference can, quite literally, make or break a company, yet it's highly unlikely that the company's executive team uses it as a key performance metric. Worse, it's possible that all of those key metrics are financial and, by definition, lagging indicators of company health.

Imagine this: People with the word *brand* in their job description typically finish a year and are assessed against shipments, market share, and their product P&L. But they are never assessed against the actual health of their brand. In practice, all this would take is the tracking of one leading indicator—difference.

Several years ago I sat with the CMO of a very large single-brand company while he shared with me his KPIs (key performance indicators). To my amazement, this accomplished marketer, inside a large, sophisticated company, was being held responsible for the brand's numerical ranking on the annual *BusinessWeek* brand study, which is basically a financial analysis. Instead of tracking brand strength, it uses a witch's brew of numbers, all of which could be increasing while the brand is going to hell. Further, his KPI was a ranking—a relative measure—so if others failed he would succeed, and vice versa. So the most senior brand leader was being held to a relative measure consisting of lagging indicators, rather than a simple, absolute leading indicator. This seems amateurish, but again, this was an accomplished marketer in a large, sophisticated company.

This is not an unusual circumstance.

Most performance metrics are designed to keep employees on the straight and narrow, not to reward them for forging a new trail. They are designed around proven paths and well-understood constructs. They are inherently short-term in nature, highly structured, financially driven, and inhospitable to difference. By definition, these metrics look backwards. They do not reward risk taking. They do not facilitate or properly incentivize innovation.

At the end of the day, performance metrics are designed to guide behavior, and they do. You reap what you sow. Where high risk meets low reward, there is little hope for difference.

ANALYSIS PARALYSIS

Large companies run on analysis. Inside these companies, analysis creates safe ground. People are expected to "know," not to "believe" or "feel." Here, analysis and data are often mistaken for "knowledge." Of course, analysis is good. As we'll discuss elsewhere, analysis gets you into the right strategic neighborhood, but it gets all of your competitors there too. The right neighborhood is insufficient. Particularly when it comes to doing different, analysis can't tell you exactly where to build your house.

I recently had a fascinating conversation with someone who manages a very large, iconic American brand. Smart and highly analytical, she had commissioned a huge amount of research that had—I argued—taken her to a completely generic positioning neighborhood. Here's the tricky part: the analysis wasn't wrong. I could neither "prove" the analysis wrong, nor "prove" my perspective right. The analysis was entirely defensible, because it was purely data driven. But it was generically correct, which just doesn't get you where you need to be in business. It's the right answer only if you don't place any value on difference.

I also see this in large technology companies. I once gave a presentation to a very large group of managers at a big, well-known tech firm. I was generally impressed by the intelligence of this fairly young group of marketers. When asked by their boss what I thought of the team, my initial response was just that—"They are a really smart, enthusiastic group of people." Then I had to add, "But there was no wisdom in the room." Young, highly intelligent, and very analytical, they "knew" marketing, but they hadn't yet built—or they failed to see the need for—the intuition and wisdom that separates great marketers from the rank and file.

It's fine to be data driven as long as you add experience-based judgment and intuition into the mix. Great strategy combines thinking and feeling, left and right brain working together, and large companies are decidedly left-brain organisms. As always, Elon Musk has an interesting perspective:

"The problem is that at a lot of big companies, process becomes a substitute for thinking. You're encouraged to behave like a little gear in a complex machine. Frankly, it allows you to keep people who aren't that smart, who aren't that creative."

One of the biggest issues I have with analysis is that it tends to be done by analysts. It usually starts at a junior level and bubbles up. In this sense, analysis is actually a surreptitious form of management from below. Also it tends to be conducted by people who believe that analysis is an absolute—you run the numbers and you get an answer. For small, routine analysis, this is not a problem, but when you are trying to guide your business forward through differentiated strategies, it's entirely the wrong approach. Difference demands more experience, judgment, and high-DQ people driving the analysis. People thinking of possibilities first, then using analysis to support, kill, or refine a unique line of thinking.

Linear thinking often gets an unfairly bad rap. Sometimes it's not the linearity that's the problem; it's the line you choose. When that line is driven by high-DQ thinking and an open mind informed by experience, the analysis is radically superior to the kind of rote, generic, bottom-up analysis that too often drives large companies ahead.

BUSINESS MODEL MYOPIA

Generally speaking, large companies want to make the most out of their business model, not change it. Even when their business is under threat, they are engineered to exploit what's already in the building. Employees are placed in roles designed to facilitate that exploitation, and those who perform best get furthest ahead. We've watched in confusion as these companies have marched in lockstep right over the cliff that was so very clearly in front of them: Kodak, Blockbuster, Borders books, and TV Guide, to be joined in the near future by companies like Sears, United, and JCPenney. Leadership at these companies obviously clings to that poisonous axiom: If we just keep doing it the same way, but better, we'll be fine. Each of these companies has faced at least one key inflection point—a point at which it wasn't too late to change—and marched right past it. If they had, embedded in their company cultures, the invitation to do something radically different, could they have survived? Even prospered?

As Peter Drucker succinctly stated: "If you want something new, you have to stop doing something old." These companies didn't value difference. They didn't see the possibilities beyond their established business models. They didn't have the high-DQ people they needed. Change is not for the weak of heart, and strategically these companies were—and are—weak of heart.

In stark contrast, look at the history of Netflix, a success story that already features several major business-model shifts. Then there's a Bill Gates story I love. It's probably part truth and part legend, but it's a great story that plays out in two acts—myopia and bravery.

Bill Gates and Microsoft lived in denial. The company that saw their business model as the physical selling of software resisted the sea change that was the internet. Resisted for far too long. Bad Bill. But one day our hero realized his company's mistake. According to folklore, upon this realization, Bill quite literally ran through the halls of Microsoft, disrupting meetings and processes, and essentially moved his company online. Good Bill.

I'm sure the real story is much more complicated, but the lesson is clear. None of the companies I listed above had—or has—a leadership team that would run through the halls demanding radical change. Instead they sit in large, expensive offices paid for by the old business model, bemoaning the changing world.

It's survival of the fittest, and they are simply not fit enough to survive.

To run at scale, large companies must develop a sustainable business model, an organizational structure, and a comprehensive rule set. Large organizations need systems, and those systems, however well-intentioned, generally function as mistake-avoidance machines rather than breakthrough-creation engines. Too often in corporate culture, mistakes are punished more loudly than successes are celebrated. Too often those who challenge the status quo are viewed as people who "need to get on board."

All of this is to say that most large companies are built on cultures, behavioral norms, and rule sets that suppress difference in the people who work for them. Knowing this, individuals with a propensity to think differently are not generally attracted to work for large companies. This cycle creates companies big in size but small in DQ. If you believe the best strategies are developed by thinking differently and encouraging opposing viewpoints, this state of affairs isn't good for business. If you believe difference is the engine room of great brands, this isn't good for business. If you believe innovation is important, this isn't good for business. If you want your people to believe they can make a difference, this isn't good for business.

In short, this isn't good for business.

Yvon Chouinard, legendary founder of Patagonia and someone uniquely grounded in the natural world, has a great take on these dynamics: "Only on the fringes of an ecosystem, those outer rings, do evolution and adaptation occur at a furious pace; the inner center of the system is where the entrenched, non-adapting species die off, doomed to failure by maintaining the status quo. Businesses go through the same cycles."

But what can we do about it? How can we ensure that large organizations encourage rather than quash difference? Like most things, it starts at the top. CEOs who value DQ build a culture, from the ground up, that supports it. These companies are led by a rare breed of visionaries: People who actively enjoy the prospect of breaking rules and carving new paths. People who want to change the world, or at least their company's part of it. These CEOs surround themselves with people who challenge their thinking. They encourage rebellion. They encourage employees to challenge leadership and themselves. There is an intellectual humility to these CEOs, a quality that makes the rest of us want to work for them. Their organizations, from top to bottom, encourage managers to bust up the status quo when it isn't working in the company's best interest. These companies use various mechanisms to encourage this, but for any mechanism to work, the difference-enhancing spirit has to be organic and it has to start at the top.

Make no mistake, in any company, creating a major cultural shift of any kind can be tough going. In a very large company, attempting to change the culture from difference-killer to difference-creator is a particularly daunting—but ultimately rewarding—task. I've watched several strong CEOs try unsuccessfully to make their organization "more entrepreneurial" or "more innovative"—enough to make me a bit skeptical about company-wide culture shifts in large organizations. Understandable, given the performance metrics, analysis paralysis, and business model myopia common among most businesses running at scale. Any attempt to graft some difference-enhancing solutions onto the typical large company structure is doomed to fail unless leaders throughout the organization are truly ready to raise their DQ. Even then, the way forward is not always clear.

YOU'RE BIG. WORK SMALL.

Business luminaries and social scientists agree: difference, creativity, innovation, and risk taking all thrive better in smaller groups. But what is the optimal size? The magic number seems to be somewhere around 150. "Dunbar's number"—named for British anthropologist Robin Dunbar—is 150. He theorized that primates have the cognitive capacity to maintain a maximum of 150 close relationships. Bill Gates thought it was around two hundred, and Richard Branson thought it was somewhere between fifty and sixty. Malcolm Gladwell wrote about this in *Tipping Point*, citing the example of Gore Associates, who refuse to house more than 150 of their people in any one facility. Navy SEAL teams consist of six platoons and around 192 personnel in total.

So what is a large company to do? Create smaller groups—custom-designed teams tasked with innovation and disruption, teams designed to look for blue oceans, zero-to-one solutions, difference-based strategies, and more.

How would you go about this? Sit down, look at your business, and see those places where difference will serve you best, where difference will make the biggest . . . difference. Start with new ventures, strategies, and brand management. Build out from there as you develop, and then start flexing your organization's DQ muscle.

These smaller groups can have an entirely disproportionate impact on a business. But they are not groups formed out of your average employee pool. They must be designed from scratch, structurally built to be high DQ, with people who probably wouldn't survive in your company's general population. Build them, then let their difference infect others. These people will cost more, occasionally cause more trouble than they seem to be worth, and challenge traditional power structures within your company. But make no mistake, they will be worth all that money and aggravation.

If Barnes & Noble had been first to sell books online, what is the delta between the position this initiative would have created and where they actually sit today? What if Blockbuster had embraced the future instead of spending years in a dream state? What if GM had created Tesla? What if Comcast had seen the writing on the wall (it was right there, in large, brightly painted colors) and built a future-proof content strategy? What if Regus had anticipated the move to a distributed workforce and created an internal version of WeWork? (If they had, maybe the rest of us wouldn't have had to put up with those awful, self-important WeWork leaders.) All of these companies were staring straight ahead, working hard within their established business definition, but perhaps an internal "difference team" would have looked to the side or around the corner and seen the opportunity.

A note of caution: A company can add custom-designed teams, but what happens when these outliers come up with brilliant ideas that challenge the status quo? Does the rest of the company have the courage to change course and run with them? How much change can a "difference team" create if they're working on the deck of an oversized, slow-moving ship destined for red oceans? Don't waste the time and money if you're not prepared to change course. Remember: these groups or teams are not designed to make things incrementally better; they are designed to make things *radically* better (and to avoid things becoming radically worse).

They are designed to make a difference.

Take a look at what Lou Gerstner did when he wanted to start the revolution at IBM years ago: he fired every communication agency IBM had in the world and hired one—Ogilvy & Mather. Before he arrived as IBM's first CEO hired from the outside, the company was allowing its various divisions to rebrand and manage themselves.

This is otherwise known as management by anarchy—weak and rarely (never) successful. He brought the company back together through broad "solutions" that only IBM could offer. In making the shift to one global advertising agency, his reasoning was simple: he wanted to show IBM's people how serious he was about unification. This was an easy, immediate, highly visible step. Smart move by a smart, uniquely successful CEO.

The idea of big companies "working small" reflects an intuitive belief that entrepreneurship is a better breeding ground for difference than is the large corporation. Of course, in many ways it has been. One problem, though: according to a 2016 article in *The Atlantic*, entrepreneurship, as measured by the rate of new-business formation, has declined in each decade since the 1970s. Millennials are currently on track to be the least entrepreneurial generation on record. The article explains, "This decline in dynamism has coincided with the rise of extraordinarily large and profitable firms that look discomfortingly like the monopolies and oligopolies of the nineteenth century." The share of all businesses held by new firms has fallen by 50 percent since 1978, and according to the Roosevelt Institute, "Markets are now more concentrated and less competitive than at any point since the Gilded Age." (By the way, the Gilded Age was the last thirty years or so of the nineteenth century. Yep, I had to google it.)

Yes, despite all the noise about Silicon Valley startups, our companies are getting bigger.

Contributing to this increase in scale, innovative thinkers attracted to the difference-incubators we call startups often find their small companies swallowed into the belly of a large corporate whale. Maybe that's fine. Maybe that's what they want in the moment—the buyout, the transition into something larger. But what happens to innovative thinkers—and their acquired products or services—inside that large company culture? As many will attest, it's unlikely to last long or end well for high-DQ products and services, or for high-DQ people.

Of course, I'm talking generalities, and there are exceptions—large companies with high DQ. To repeat, in these organizations the call for difference comes from the very top: the rare high-DQ CEO. If you're not lucky enough to work for one of these people, be warned: whatever your personal DQ may be on your way into a large company, it likely will be significantly lower on your way out. I've seen this play out too many times.

And what about the other end of the spectrum: the truly small company? Companies with fewer than twenty people account for more than 60 percent of all US firms and employ about 20 million people. Is this a high-DQ playground? We all get caught up in the tech-startup fairy tales, but what about the millions of small businesses struggling to get ahead in more traditional, analog categories? It's easy to forget this, sitting here in tech-saturated San Francisco, but in the greater scheme of things, companies that set out to change the world by doing something truly different are the exception, not the rule. Most small companies operate in existing markets, using existing approaches. Their focus is not creating difference; it's staying afloat. Their mantra is not "Move fast and break things"; it's "Stay alive." For small businesses, this day-to-day struggle for survival is a difference-dampener that, realistically, won't ever change.

But medium and large companies can change. They can find ways to work with their scale, foster innovation, enhance difference, and actively challenge their status quo. It's not easy, but surely it's worth the investment.

LET'S BACK UP A STEP. IS BIGGER ACTUALLY BETTER?

Financial markets tell us that bigger is better—but is it? Surely there's a point of diminishing return.

When I worked at Kellogg's, I was fortunate enough to spend some time with a fascinating guy named Bill LaMothe, our much-loved chairman. At the time, our competitors were acquiring new companies at a rapid clip. Bill told me he was being criticized by the press for not following suit. He wasn't necessarily against the idea, but he'd seen nothing worth acquiring, nothing that wouldn't dilute Kellogg's focus. Bill faced so much external pressure that he eventually decided he must be in the wrong. Maybe he'd better get out there and buy something? Thankfully, about then, all around us, massive mergers and acquisitions started to fail, one after the other. Within a few months, Bill LaMothe was being lauded for his focus.

Personally, I think the general concept of a "holding company," wherein a parent company owns separate businesses with little actual synergy or scale economy between them, is just bad strategy. Bad strategy created by financial pressure to grow, corporate greed, and executive hubris. As a stockholder, I would rather invest in three well-run, uniquely focused companies, believing they will outperform one holding company running three nonsynergistic businesses. Being good three times doesn't beat being great once.

Focus allows for difference. Difference is our friend.

Of course, companies can grow very large while maintaining focus and difference. They can change and invent as they grow. The aforementioned Disney and Netflix are great examples, as are Apple and Walmart. *The Wall Street Journal*'s list of best-managed companies is a great reference, as it's essentially based on thirty-four indicators driven by the principles of management guru Peter Drucker. In 2019, the top five were all technology companies, led by Amazon—which pretty much blew everyone else away, particularly on the innovation front. Amazon files more patent apps than any-one else on the list, and also abandons more—both great signs of a constantly evolving strategy. The resurgent Microsoft, led so well by Satya Nadella, came second, followed by Apple, Alphabet, and Cisco.

Personally, I think search-engine-based financial success at Alphabet hides some debatable strategic moves. Alphabet is a highly diversified nondiversified company. At its core, this is a verbal and visual search and advertising company. At its core, this company is incredibly focused. But outside that core, with the exception of the very intelligent purchase of YouTube (now the second-largest search engine), they have wasted a lot of time and a ton of money everywhere else. Why? Because they're not really focused on lever-aging their difference.

Even an organization as big and successful as Alphabet has opportunity cost. As an example, look at YouTube. With benefit of hindsight (I know, I hate it when people do this), one might argue that the success of Netflix was fully available to YouTube. How is it that people who understand search so deeply don't seem to understand how to architect a site? Lacking the necessary strategic discipline and focus, Google (which created Alphabet in its 2015 restructuring) simply did not put enough thought, time, or money into this very important strategic opportunity.

Enough. As someone who is constitutionally incapable of run-ning a truly large company, I feel a bit hypocritical criticizing them (though that obviously hasn't stopped me). Let's end this criticism with a clear and concise summary:

When scale meets cultural rigidity, difference dies.

When you understand the importance of difference—in busi-ness, in solving for global challenges, in life in general—you under-stand the urgent need to keep difference alive. To blend thinking and feeling, analysis and intuition. To seek work-arounds within our large-scale institutions. To raise our collective DQ, in our schools, in our religious and cultural institutions, in our companies, no matter their size.

How do we do this? You tell me. When it comes to our difference-dampeners, it should be very clear that I'm better at illuminating the opportunity than at creating solutions. I'm defining the gap, hoping some of you will fill it.

"Do not go where the path may lead, go instead where there is no path and leave a trail."
—Ralph Waldo Emerson

CHAPTER 6

OUR SELVES

"If you are always trying to be normal, you will never know how amazing you can be."

—Maya Angelou

At the age of fourteen, with my parents and brother, I emigrated from Scotland to Canada. My father had a James Bond accent that people loved, and my mother had the most proper English accent you could imagine. Their two boys had the worst possible Glaswegian accents. Have you ever watched a film shot in Scotland and wondered, "What the hell did he just say?" Well, my accent was much harder to understand than that actor's. Not only that, but my mother sent me off to my first day at school—the toughest school in town—in a standard Scottish school uniform: a shirt and tie. Guys in my class were fighting to be first to beat the crap out of the weird new kid who wouldn't speak properly.

Worse, I was ahead of the curve academically (not hard to do at this school), so the administration tried to push me up a couple of grades. Thankfully, my parents agreed only to one. Still, I spent the next several years as an immature, painfully thin math geek with a funny accent. How did I survive? Like so many kids, I did my best to blend in.

The worst of the bullying behavior was generally reserved for others, but only because I happened to be a good athlete, so I had large friends. Also, I smoothed out my accent and I kept my academic strength under the radar while pouring myself into athletics, because that's where I fit in best. In general, I hid my difference and, with the exception of one amazing, eccentric old history teacher named Mr. Grass, everyone let me.

A childhood spent trying to fit in became an early adulthood focused on the same. As I started to succeed in my business career, I became responsible for larger groups of often older people, so I tried desperately to look and sound older than I was. I even grew a pretty embarrassing beard at one point. It all served me pretty well, and I became a CEO by the age of thirty-five. But I was acting the part. Along the way, I'd lost track of my difference.

I also saw this dynamic at play with my own kids. My son was an accomplished and confident athlete who always walked his own path. Sitting at the top of the school social pyramid, he saw no need to try to fit in, partly because of who he was and partly because the world bent itself toward him. He had all the cultural capital he needed.

My daughter has always been unique in ways I both love and respect. She didn't have the cultural currency of sports to call on, but when you combine self-confidence with an abundance of empathy, as she did, you become someone other kids want to be around. She did not, however, walk through childhood unscathed.

In middle school, my daughter stood up for a kid who was being bullied by a group of mean girls. In retaliation, they launched a campaign to bring my daughter down a peg. It was tough to watch her repel the attack at first, then compromise to get herself out of the line of fire. Pinned down by the school's queen bee, she just didn't have the energy to stay her own course. How many kids her age would?

My point is this: sometimes we ourselves are the biggest dampeners of our difference.

Eventually my daughter rediscovered her unique voice, and I'm now the proud father of a son who continues to be his own person and a daughter who, as a teacher, encourages kids to explore and celebrate their difference.

Clearly, I too rediscovered my difference, and now I'm encouraging you to do the same. In order to do different in business, we need to eradicate the difference-dampeners within ourselves.

To do so, we'll need to push up against some deeply ingrained human tendencies.

THE INSTINCT TO CONFORM

In the 1950s, psychologist Solomon Asch conducted a study testing the human tendency toward conformity. He placed subjects in a room with a set of actors. The group was then asked to say which of three lines on one card matched the length of one line on another card. As a group, the actors gave erroneous—often significantly erroneous—answers. Guess what? The subjects tended to conform to the group answer. Normal error in this experiment was around 1 percent. But when faced with a group unanimously agreeing upon a wrong answer, the subjects' error rate shot up to 37 percent.

Unsurprising conclusion—we conform.

We're influenced by some pretty powerful human, operating-system-level motivations. Back when our tribe was roaming the plains looking for food, standing out could be a life-or-death affair. Today, standing out invites attack and ridicule, which can threaten our mental and physical health. In a low-DQ workplace, standing out—in the wrong way, at least—can be dangerous to our careers. So it makes sense that we approach difference with caution.

But Asch's study revealed something else about conformity: a quarter of his subjects were uninfluenced by the actors' unanimously wrong response, consistently ignoring it and answering correctly. Does this mean 25 percent of us have a high DQ? Does it mean that a second group of subjects who agreed with the actors almost all the time have lower DQ? Voilà! We have some kind of DQ normal curve.

Yes, as a species we are social animals with a distinct tendency to follow the crowd. We join lines. We join clubs. We act in ways that (we hope) will make people like us. We wear clothes to suit the moment. We set goals that align with agreed-upon measures for status and success. Research has shown that we even change our speech patterns to match those of the people around us.

Or the majority of us do, at least.

In *Sapiens*, historian Yuval Noah Harari posits that Homo sapiens came to dominate this planet largely because our species can cooperate flexibly in large numbers. This ability to cooperate in large numbers originates in a unique ability to believe in concepts that exist only in our imaginations, concepts such as gods, countries, money, and laws. Harari sees all large-scale human cooperation systems—including religions, political structures, corporations, and legal institutions—as owing their existence to this uniquely human capacity for fiction.

It's important to note that these systems simply won't work unless people conform to them. Without mass conformity, they are useless constructs. Yes, sapiens have a unique ability to imagine, to believe in constructs that don't actually exist. But we also have an innate need to fit in, an urge to conform, without which this world we live in would be much more chaotic than it already is.

Like it or not, conformity is an integral, possibly essential, part of human existence. Even an anarchist group conforms to a set of ideals. Add to this innate human characteristic the external, often intense social pressure to fit in, and it's not surprising that true individualism is pretty rare.

In researching conformity I read heartbreaking articles and blogs written by people who knew they didn't fit in and, worse, were made to feel smaller because of it. Knowing you are different is one thing. Being actively shunned and humiliated for that difference is another thing entirely.

If this were a Marvel blockbuster movie, people with high DQ would be the mutants who learned to hide their unique powers to avoid persecution, even when those differences could benefit all of humankind. Unfortunately it's not a movie. It's a reality in which people hide the differences that could save us all.

The wise philosopher known as Dr. Seuss has something important to say about this: "Today you are you, that is truer than true. There is no one alive who is youer than you."

All of this brings us back to our paradox: we celebrate high-DQ people who have broken into the upper echelons of fame in business, politics, the arts, and entertainment, but we are ruthless dampeners of difference within ourselves.

Our craving for acceptance, our desire to be liked—nowhere do we see this more clearly than on social media. We post our photographs and broadcast our thoughts in the spirit of self-expression, but we do so in the hope that our expressions will be "liked" by others. What happens when we calculate the value of our life experiences through the number of likes accumulated rather than the inherent pleasure of the experience itself?

This need to be approved of and admired by others—even those we don't know—makes no sense to me. When did regular people start marketing themselves—their lives, their activities, their families—to an audience? Faking travel photographs to impress their followers? Hiring professional photographers to increase their likes? Soliciting, even buying, followers to appear more popular?

We're raising a whole generation of people who feel that an experience isn't complete until it's shared on social media. They're hooked on gaining the approval of complete strangers.

I saw this in action on vacation recently. There we were, in an absolutely beautiful tropical setting, watching the sun set over the ocean. On the beach were two women in their twenties, wearing identical outfits, assuming fun poses, taking one photograph after another of each other. They were so intent on their appearance in the "golden hour" light, they were shooting photos with a concrete hotel in the background, oblivious to the sunset painting its vibrant colors over the ocean. I can only hope that their audience, unaware of the natural beauty that lurked close by, liked the hell out of their poses.

You've got to wonder what this obsession with "likes" will do to our collective DQ.

Yes, conformity has its function—we humans must band together for protection and to accomplish essential tasks. Yes, formalized groups create much-needed structure, from small teams in companies, to cities, to countries, to international organizations. That said, some of the worst moments in human history grew out of a leader's ability to manipulate group conformity and leverage it for their own purposes. When a mass of people moves in the wrong direction, the conforming many can drown out the objections of the few who dare to stand up against the wrong.

Peter Icke put this thought much more dramatically: "The human race is a herd. Here we are, unique, eternal aspects of consciousness with an infinity of potential, and we have allowed ourselves to become an unthinking, unquestioning blob of conformity and uniformity. A herd. Once we concede to the herd mentality, we can be controlled and directed by a tiny few. And we are."

The same can be said within business: the conforming many can drown out the high-DQ few, to the detriment of us all.

The experiments of Solomon Asch suggest that some of us are born with a very high resistance to conformity while others show up with very low resistance, and most of us fall somewhere in the middle of the curve. No matter where we line up, from the moment we're born until we finally learn not to care so much, a range of very powerful influences work to suppress our DQ.

At some point, though, we need to ask: Exactly how much of this pressure to conform is self-created? How much is a natural part of being human? How much is visited upon us by our institutions early in our lives? How much is enforced by the sometimes-harsh reality of earning a paycheck? At some stage in our personal development, we need to take responsibility for our direction and push back against the pressure to conform. We need to better understand and promote the benefits of being different—for ourselves, the companies we work for, and the culture we live in.

Ultimately, I believe we can train DQ. We can work against the limitations of conformity and increase the DQ of our people, our organizations, and our society.

As I write this, we are all sheltering in place because of COVID-19. In order to beat this virus, we need to conform. In this sense, conformity is a good thing. We simply need to agree to follow a set of rules imposed by health officials. Most of us do so, but some of us resist. They resist because some idiots in powerful positions modeled it. Because it became a political statement. Still conformity in some ways, but conformity to a highly dangerous worldview. This is a virus that is killing a lot of people. If you don't properly value your own life, you probably don't properly value the lives of the people around you. This is a time for conformity. Wear a mask. If you must, show your independence with a message written on your mask.

On the other hand, when it comes to addressing the complex, multilayered impact of this pandemic, we need difference—unique, high-DQ solutions. In the US, at the national level at least, so far we have seen very little outside-the-box thinking. We've now seen two federal aid packages approved, and there's not a single new idea in sight. We allocate money but don't fundamentally change a thing. When you look at the breakdown of allocations, they're heavily skewed to big business, not to the people who need it most.

This pandemic is a stress test, a time to see which systems are broken and which need to be built. The US response to the pandemic has been a total shambles, while other countries were systemically better suited to mount a centrally coordinated response. While people in the United States have been left to fend for themselves, universal health care and worker protections in other countries have kept the most vulnerable citizens safe. Yes, the callous lack of leadership exhibited by Donald Trump was a huge part of the problem, but let's face it, as a country we're just not organized to deal with this kind of crisis. Let's note that later, when it came down to simply throwing a lot of money and economic muscle at vaccine development and distribution, America fared much better. Money and muscle are our wheelhouse. Systemic protection of vulnerable people is most definitely not.

Crisis creates opportunity. If ever there was a time to fix some of the most broken inner workings of our country, this is it. But can we learn? Are we willing to look at things that worked in other places and embrace them? Can we change?

I know this is easy to say and much tougher to do, but this pandemic points a very bright light into the future. This could be our wake-up call, nationally and globally. But only if we act differently. Only if nations cooperate, share the science, and act as one.

Once the dust settles, will we be thinking, working, or acting any differently? Please let it be so.

MAYBE WE'RE ALL JUST CULT MEMBERS?

As I read articles and studies on the subject of societal confor-mity, I was struck by the idea that cults are, in many ways, a highly focused form of conformity and control. Perhaps understanding the dynamics of cult membership gives us a very concentrated look into this pressure to conform.

For starters, are all cults led by an individual with high DQ but filled with people with low DQ? Could a person with high DQ ever survive inside a cult?

Dr. Janja Lalich is an author and professor of sociology who focuses on cult groups, specializing in charismatic authority, power relations, ideology, coercion, and social control. I found her work fairly easy for a layman like me to understand. Dr. Lalich describes a sort of "self-sealed system" and outlines four dimensions of a cult:

1. charismatic authority, which is pretty self-apparent and fits everyone's cult stereotype
2. a transcendent belief system, which offers a complete explanation to the members
3. systems of control, involving a set of rules, regulations, and procedures
4. systems of influence, essentially described as the expected peer and leadership pressure

It strikes me that as most of us go through a "non-cult life," we face very similar dimensions, but in a less intense form. We join groups, often led by our more charismatic peers and influencers. We "follow" charismatic celebrities. As we grow older and these groups become formal, the systems of control and influence also become more formal and set. All groups, from countries to compa-nies, have some form of belief system, whether explicit or implicit.

What can the model of cult behavior teach us about difference in business?

Traditionally we view cults as unhealthy, in that they are made up of people who believe deeply, perhaps fanatically, in something that simply isn't true. They are often isolated from people outside the cult, and often asked to shed their non-cult life—past, present, and future.

Kind of sounds like a startup to me.

To be fair, perhaps a startup is a "healthy cult," in that it's characterized by a small group of people who believe, somewhat fanatically, in an idea. Generally a new idea. Generally a true idea. But, while the idea may be true, the real question is whether or not the idea has the potential that the team so fervently believes it has.

In a different area of the business sector, we hear talk of "cult brands." What does it take for a brand to reach this status? Cult brands are highly differentiated and therefore adopted as a form of social identification. They are products and services that we don't just use, but join. We participate in them and they give us back a sense of belonging. Harley-Davidson and Apple are classic examples of brands that have engendered this level of emotional intensity among their followers. Also consider brands such as *Game of Thrones*, Trader Joe's, In-N-Out, Peloton, and Philz Coffee. Or one of my personal favorites at the moment, Allbirds. Damn, those shoes are comfortable!

At the end of the day, as human beings, we all want to belong to something. Our search for belonging inevitably drives a certain level of conformity, and marketplace conformity can actually be very good for business. Joining a cult represents the extreme end of this need, but we seek belonging in other ways—belonging among family and friends, belonging to causes, places, and brands—all at various settings on the emotional health and intensity dial.

In this sense, good marketing plays both sides of the conformity game. I'm urging marketers to do something uniquely compelling, so large groups of people will notice, join, and follow them.

THE DARK SIDE OF DIFFERENCE

As much as I would love to see marketers embrace this idea of difference, I'd be much, much happier if human beings would embrace it.

I wrote this book about something I know—marketing. However, it wouldn't feel complete without recognizing the awful track record we humans have with "difference." Countless horrors have resulted from people conforming to a harmful social narrative when they should have differed forcefully from the misguided norm. In a supposedly civilized, advanced, global society, instead of embracing and celebrating difference, we tend to polarize, attack, and punish. Why?

Difference can lead to classification, and the human mind seems to have a hard time classifying without ranking. When two things are different, we tend to automatically think of one as better and the other as worse. Difference gets converted to a statement of superior versus inferior. Fit versus unfit. This is applied to individuals and groups, to gender, race, ethnicity, religion, sexual orientation, nationality, and so many other classifications. It's also applied to ideas. But difference doesn't need to be vertical. Difference can be a completely horizontal concept, with no values or judgment attached.

Different does not mean better or worse; it means different.

It deeply saddens me to see how, as human beings, all together on a tiny planet in a vast universe, we see difference as a flaw to be masked rather than a natural feature of life to be explored and celebrated. How much would the world change if we simply began thinking of difference, well . . . differently?

That's my ask.

Be different. Do different. Love different.

"Conformity is the jailer of freedom and the enemy of growth."
—John F. Kennedy

PART III

THE REAL-WORLD CREATION OF DIFFERENCE

"Being the best is great, you're number one. Being unique is greater, you're the only one."

—Anonymous

CHAPTER 7

FINDING DIFFERENCE IN THREE BUSINESS SCENARIOS

"Two roads diverged in a wood, and I—
I took the one less traveled by,
And that has made all the difference."
—Robert Frost

Welcome back to the land of marketing. Let's pause for a moment and take stock. Where are we in the case for difference? We've covered the following points:

- Difference is the engine room of strong businesses and brands.
- Any idiot can be different. You must find difference that's actually compelling to your audience. Difference that can create competitive advantage.
- Your job is to find your differentiated advantage, then to commit yourself to it, to the exclusion of other

opportunities. If you can't stay focused on your differentiated advantage, you will drift. If you drift, you will lose.

- Once you have found your difference, create a strategy that is culturally noisy. When you build a position of differentiated advantage, you have a good launching pad for a disruptive, maybe even counterintuitive, attention-grabbing point of view.

- Diversity is a path to difference. Embrace diversity as a source of competitive advantage. Please.

- Many difference-dampeners—from parents, to schools, to religious institutions, to our companies, to our own hardwiring as humans—threaten our DQ. We need to push back against these forces to make space for difference.

- Make no mistake, with difference comes risk. What's your risk tolerance? What's the risk tolerance of the people you work for? To leverage difference, you might need to raise your DQ and theirs.

- Or maybe you just need to look at the evidence. The case for difference is well supported by experienced observation, social scientists, business luminaries, and data. Maybe the greatest risk of all is failing to take a risk?

Clearly, I think the case for difference is inarguable, but it's what you think that matters most. Are you ready to take the difference pledge?

If you're committed to differentiated advantage, then the process itself is quite simple. To review, whether you're positioning a person, a place, an idea, a product, a service, or a company, the steps are the same:

Step 1: List the ways in which your "thing" is different.

Step 2: Select the difference that contains the greatest competitive advantage and audience appeal.

Of course, like most things in life, it's not as easy as it sounds. The complexity comes not in the process, but in its real-world application.

With this in mind, let's begin the hunt for differentiated advantage, in three common business scenarios: embedded difference, discovered difference, and created difference.

SCENARIO #1: EMBEDDED DIFFERENCE

In this scenario, you have a business that was built around a true difference. The more deeply the difference is embedded, the better. Here, the difference is obvious, and it's really just up to the marketer to stay focused and consistent (often easier said than done). For the marketer, the question is, How can you consistently bring that difference to life in a compelling, culturally relevant, and intelligently disruptive way?

Some examples of embedded difference to consider:

I've mentioned **Southwest** and **Walmart** a couple times already. Let me tell you why: they're great illustrations of the advantage of a deeply embedded difference. In both cases, the entire operation was built, from the ground up, to deliver a lower-cost product to the customer. Most competitive airlines or retailers would have to press operational restart, or accept unacceptably low margins, in order to challenge their difference. In other words, if you want to go up against them on price, you will lose.

Now, this is nuance, but notice that neither of these companies stopped at just price. Southwest does everything they can to make the experience of air travel seem accessible and fun. If you look at Walmart a bit more closely, you'll see they don't promise the lowest price in town; they promise "everyday low prices." They seek to reduce the complexity and pressure of constantly seeking the lowest promotional price on a specific item and offer a much simpler proposition to their shoppers. Both companies uniquely simplify, and thereby they reassure.

Such deeply embedded difference can be an extremely powerful business asset, but it's not insurmountable. Look at Boeing, which felt a profound sense of competitive safety until a bunch of European governments got together to create a deep-pocketed competitor called Airbus. Or FedEx, a pioneer company that simplified an incredibly complex process and became shorthand for delivery, only to find that, over time, their business could still be eroded by UPS. Yes, FedEx lost their focus along the way (can you spell Kinko's?), but one might have expected their business model to be much less permeable than has actually been the case.

Netflix was originally built to sell or rent DVDs at a time when the future of this format was in serious doubt. They redefined the word *pivot* as they changed what they did without losing sight of their single ambition: to be our personal entertainment content library. First they focused on DVDs. Then renting. Then subscriptions. Then streaming. These are clearly huge changes, but all grounded in a single idea. Netflix resisted any temptation to extend into areas that didn't serve that central idea. If we think of that idea as a pipeline through time, we see they've both stayed inside the pipe and made a hell of a noise by banging on its inside edges. Yes, Disney+ may challenge Netflix for audience, but at this point only Amazon seems capable of challenging their point of difference.

Venice is completely and utterly unique. Whether you love the idea of Venice or not, you know exactly what the idea is and that you can find it in only one place. Sadly, its difference comes with a price. As I write, Venice is flooded, again.

Four Seasons sets the standard for luxury hotels and resorts. Yes, there are better individual hotels and better locations to be found, but it's very hard to find better service, and Four Seasons has capitalized on that difference. Their name has become synonymous with luxury and service, even among well-heeled travelers who might stay elsewhere. While their difference is deeply culturally embedded, it is service based and therefore inherently more vulnerable than the deeply embedded operational differences owned by others.

SCENARIO #2: DISCOVERED DIFFERENCE

In the second scenario, there is difference to be found in the business, but the business itself isn't built around a deeply embedded difference. Often a business walks away from its difference, or simply loses focus. This usually happens gradually, one small step at a time. At some point, those small steps lead to a harmful detour. Other times, the business never really recognized the unique attributes it possessed. Brands are built from the inside, so the first task here is to find the difference that will best guide and inspire the supporting organization, so that they can, in turn, guide and inspire their external audience.

A story about quality and some examples to consider:

First, a personal story. It may seem a bit off topic, but I think it's instructive. The idea of small steps that add up to a major detour reminds me of my very first marketing position. Armed with my first credit card and wearing my first real suit, I was the very picture of a self-important assistant brand manager. Like any young brand manager out to impress, I found a way to lower the cost of my product without lowering any quality perceptions among our customers. My bosses were impressed, and off we went. But after we put the reformulated product on the shelves, business dropped like a rock. What the hell? Highly frustrated, I went back into the files, and after a lot of digging I learned that I was just the latest in a long line of ambitious brand assistants, all of whom had sought to impress through some cost-reduction scheme. Though my change was not significant, all those insignificant changes added up, and I was the one who blithely drove the car off the cliff.

I tell this story because I think there's always a larger picture to consider, one that is often missed. Most businesses are run intelligently. Though it certainly happens, most leadership teams do not make major decisions that hurt their business in a significant way. But small decisions can add up. Whether it's product quality, protecting your difference, or maintaining positioning integrity, a series of small decisions can take you off track just as surely as one major decision. Small decisions are not always as small as they seem, so approach them with care.

Back to a few illustrations of discovered difference. A few years ago, NBC's **TODAY** show was rapidly losing viewers to ABC's *Good Morning America*. *GMA* had decided to build a light, entertaining way for viewers to start their day. With great chemistry between the talent and quick repartee, it popped. Now losing the ratings game, *TODAY* started to imitate what they saw as a winning formula. But this was not who they were. They weren't built for that approach; they were built for a more serious brand of journalism. Asked to build a "positioning strategy" for *TODAY*, our task was to convince them to play from strength rather than weakness, and to find a way to bring that difference to life in a consistently compelling way for the viewer. From a marketing perspective, *TODAY* needed to frame up a clear choice for the audience. Did people want to eat meat or snack on popcorn? Was the audience into real news or a morning version of *Entertainment Tonight*? Of course, this choice wasn't totally fair to *GMA*, but that's marketing.

The *TODAY* difference was right there all along; they just needed to be true to it and to position themselves around it in a way their audience would find compelling. After a few long months, *TODAY* regained the ratings lead.

Best Buy won the battle against other electronic retailers, but it was losing the war against the internet. As long as electronics were treated as the shiny object and prices were easy to compare, they were inevitably going to lose that war. We suggested to Best Buy that, in the current retail environment, their difference didn't lie in the selling of shiny objects; it lay in service. We suggested that the more unique opportunity was to position Best Buy around the services that surround the shiny object: selecting the right device for your specific needs, integrating it into your life, then maintaining it. Led by their Geek Squad (the brand catalyst that made this idea feel tangible), made much more visible in a revised store layout, and ably supported by their Blue Shirts, Best Buy has done a pretty masterful job of holding the line in a very tough marketplace.

IHOP had been losing share for years. By the time we got on board, they had lost their focus completely. Why in the world would a restaurant named the International House of Pancakes shift their focus to dinner? But that's what they had done. They'd developed a menu filled with entrees no one expected them to cook (including tilapia) and no one wanted to buy. Even worse, these menu items had created a separate (expensive) operation in the restaurant. You could have jumped up on a table and sung show tunes at IHOP in the evening, and your only audience would have been the cook and a couple of servers. If IHOP couldn't win the breakfast battle, we argued, they had no reason to be in business. They needed to regain breakfast leadership, emotionally and intellectually, even if they didn't actually lead in terms of market share. We wanted them to go all the way: breakfast + brunch (not lunch) + breakfast for dinner (brinner) + a late-night breakfast. This way, IHOP could give people something they couldn't get anywhere else. We failed to convince them to make this radical move on the operational side, but they embraced the breakfast focus from a positioning and communication perspective, and the business turned around. Operationally, I still see this as a missed opportunity, but maybe it will still happen?

Levi's is a cautionary tale that shows what happens when you pretend to be something you're not. As a brand, Levi's failed to understand the difference between marketer's stimulus and marketplace response. Desperate to be "cool" among a younger, hipper, more urban audience that wanted nothing to do with them, Levi's tried to act young, hip, and cool. Match the stimulus with the desired response—simple, right? Wrong. In the US, Levi's is seen as authentic, rugged, individualistic. Rather than chasing trends, they needed to find a modern-day expression of their true brand values. When you try to be something you're not, you're highly unlikely to be unique, and you're playing from weakness instead of strength. Instead, find the best possible cultural interpretation of your unique self and execute the hell out of it.

The same could be said of the **History Channel**. Hard to believe, but we were asked to figure out their positioning strategy. Isn't it pretty damn obvious? The *History* Channel? They should have been a shining example of embedded difference. But at that time their two top-rated shows were called *Ax Men* and *Ice Road Truckers*, and leadership didn't want to be "limited" by a focus on history. We argued that their mission was to make history entertaining and fascinating, but they said no. Of course, smarter people took over at some point, followed the mission more closely, and turned them back toward their unique, true home. Yes, they could achieve isolated ratings success with other types of programming, but surely the History Channel can only truly succeed in any sustained manner by bringing history to life in new and entertaining ways.

A couple of these examples illustrate the more difficult, two-part path to difference in this scenario. Discovering and defining your differentiated advantage is challenging enough, but you must then have the courage to follow the path demanded by that difference. IHOP and the History Channel each had only one clear path to success. It seems almost impossible that they didn't realize this. But the implications of that level of focus scared them away. Scared them into chasing business in places that had nothing whatsoever to do with who they are and why they exist. Again I ask: What's riskier—a weak decision to wander aimlessly over a seemingly broad landscape, or a strong decision to drive forward with a singular focus?

SCENARIO #3: CREATED DIFFERENCE

In this scenario, the brand has no meaningful difference. It's not embedded. It's not waiting to be uncovered. It's just . . . not there. The marketer therefore needs to create a strong and differentiating point of view for the business to embrace and come to own. Weird as it may seem, the marketer has to make something up! This scenario is the most difficult of the three, as the difference is purely a marketing construct, a unique perspective, a creation of the imagination. For all of these reasons, it can also be the most personally rewarding for the marketer. Let's take a quick look at some examples, to bring this scenario to life. Always keep in mind that created difference is about invention, so the differentiating idea is competitively vulnerable, particularly during the time between when it is introduced and when it becomes "owned."

In the first two scenarios, it's pretty clear where you need to look for difference, but not in this case. Since this is an act of creation, there are no real limits, so where the hell do you begin? You can start by considering the dynamics of your category: What "rules" can you break? Consider the audience: What irritates them and how can you help? Consider your competitors: What are they doing, and how can you do the opposite? Peter Thiel likes to ask this question:

"What important truth do very few people agree with you on?"—another challenging but possibly productive way to find difference.

Remember, you're looking for a point of view that is culturally noisy. Disruptive. Counterintuitive if possible. When competitors are complex and additive in approach, find a more minimalist, subtractive approach. If they are loud and energetic, embrace a point of view that is slow and quiet. Find the category zig, then create the brand-positioning zag.

This scenario is challenging on several levels. It takes imagination to come up with the idea in the first place. Just as important, it takes nerve to see it through. It takes organizational bravery. Created difference is a really tough sell for an organization that is naturally risk avoidant, as most certainly are. Because it's a creation, the organization will be full of less-imaginative people who think their ideas are better than yours. In short, you will most surely be second-guessed, right up to the moment your idea starts to work.

Also, successfully creating difference through a unique POV takes great communication partners. While the core strategy team rightfully gets credit for creating the Dove brand position, it was really Ogilvy & Mather who made it famous. The same could be said of the success of Axe, and this is certainly true when it comes to Old Spice (more on that soon). If you are embarking on the path of creating difference, execution can be even more important than strategy, so don't underestimate the importance—or rarity—of truly brand- and business-changing communication. Do not take a step on this path unless you are 100 percent sure you have this caliber of partner working on your behalf.

Creating a uniquely disruptive POV is absolutely the best way to create equally unique and disruptive marketing communication, but it's no guarantee. Assume you will only get one shot at making your strategy work, and don't start until you're sure that you have a highly unique, disruptive, compelling, on-position campaign firmly in hand and ready to go. This is important, and counterintuitive for most, so let me repeat: work with your communication partner, but do not spend a cent until you have something truly brilliant. Trust me, this one-time opportunity is worth the wait. Your agency can do it. If they can't, find someone who can. This is why truly stand-out advertising is so rare in America: rather than waiting until they have something brilliant, marketers tend to run with the best marketing content their agency can come up with in the time available.

Okay, enough warnings. Here are a few examples of created difference:

Target was losing the price war against Walmart, and they recognized a dead-end street when they saw one. As I write, they are celebrating the twentieth anniversary of the Design for All program, which started with designer Michael Graves and expanded over time to a long list of partnerships. In short, this program brought name designers into the Target store while maintaining the kind of pricing that the Target audience needed. It was an attempt to separate Target from Walmart, through a marketing program that became much more. When you look closely, the actual bottom-line contribution of this program is a lot less than you might expect, but that's not really the point. Design for All became famous as "cheap chic," and it was the catalyst that drove a clear, tangible differentiated advantage for the brand. In other words, it wasn't just words—you could see, feel, and buy the products that were spawned by this idea. It created a brand point of view that pulled Target apart from Walmart in a way that the Walmart culture could never really match.

I would argue that we created a similar opportunity for **JCPenney** several years ago, when we pushed them to embrace the idea of "fit." Competing against retailers whose business model forces customers to pull apparel off the rack and hope for the best, JCP was uniquely positioned to add a tailor to a store, shine up their dressing rooms, and offer a highly underserved audience the opportunity to have clothes that actually fit, which, research had shown, turned out to be women's number one wish in clothing. Add mannequins and merchandising material that features all sorts of body shapes, sizes, and colors, throw in a great ad campaign, and away you go. You may be right in thinking, *A positioning strategy like this won't save them,* but we'll never know. Sadly, internal leadership changed and politics got in the way, and today JCP's strongest message remains "On sale this week."

How about the rebirth of **Old Spice**? Old, sadly out of date, and faced with the success of Axe, Old Spice moved its audience focus younger and told men to get their swagger back. Manly men were entertained. More importantly, their partners were entertained. The marketplace talked about Old Spice's award-winning, culturally noisy advertising campaign, and we all witnessed a completely improbable brand turnaround. Yet the only thing that really changed was the brand's worldview. The "Man Your Man Could Smell Like" campaign was created by a very brave P&G brand group and, not surprisingly, by a great ad agency, Wieden+Kennedy. Anyone who says they saw this turnaround coming is delusional.

More recently, I've had the opportunity to look into the premium ice cream market. The **Ben & Jerry's** position, true and unique, was "Joy for the Belly and Soul." It was perfect, until they changed it. On the other hand, the more serious **Häagen-Dazs** brand took up an "Adult Indulgence" position brought to its limit in a sexy campaign in Europe. But then they too decided to tone things down. While I don't pretend to know the details, both companies seem to have backed away from highly unique and culturally noisy brand positions. Then in 2019, **Halo Top**, a US brand I'd never heard of, decided to differentiate itself with a dark, hilariously adult point of view. For anyone who thinks a category dictates how you position your brand, you have to check out the Halo Top "Ice Cream for Adults" campaign, created by agency 72andSunny. While Ben &

Jerry's and Häagen-Dazs found their difference within themselves, the Halo Top difference was an act of pure construction.

Like Target, Axe, Old Spice, and the Dove and Corona stories mentioned earlier, Halo Top is zigging purely because everyone else was zagging. To the marketer, these are magical creations: something entirely different and totally counterintuitive, created out of nothing.

No matter which of the three business scenarios you're working in, think of it this way: a strong brand, like a strong person, has a strong and unique point of view. This strong point of view must provide a service to its audience. It must be provocative and therefore culturally noisy. You should be able to write a short white paper on it. It could be a T-shirt your audience would gladly wear: Design for all. Beauty comes from within. Life's a beach.

In the first two scenarios, difference is found in the thing we want to market. We construct a strong point of view around that compelling difference. We market a differentiated point of view grounded in the thing. Whether it's embedded or discovered, in these scenarios a real difference creates and informs a differentiated point of view.

In the third scenario, our thing has no inherent difference, so we search for and create a uniquely compelling point of view that, over time, can become our brand's difference. In turn, this created difference starts guiding everything we do, to the point where, as much as possible, our brand comes to own this POV. In this scenario, a differentiated point of view creates and informs an idea that becomes a real business difference.

Now that we've explored the scenarios in which you'll be looking for differentiated advantage, it's time to jump into a five-point plan for creating it. Be warned: while simple to explain, creating differentiated advantage can be very challenging in practice.

*"If I'm going to sing like someone else,
then I don't need to sing at all."*

—Billie Holiday

CHAPTER 8

HOW TO CREATE DIFFERENTIATED ADVANTAGE: A PROCESS

"If you want something you've never had, you must be willing to do something you've never done."
—Thomas Jefferson

Okay, you're ready for it, right? Finally, here's the five-step process for creating differentiated positioning strategies:

1. Who is your audience?
2. What makes you different?
3. Of these differences, which will your audience find most compelling?
4. Of these compelling differences, which might yield the highest competitive advantage?
5. Of this short list of compelling differentiated advantages, which seems most . . .

- culturally noisy?
- simple?
- tangible?
- sustainable?

Let's walk through each of these steps in a bit more detail.

STEP 1: KNOW YOUR AUDIENCE.

This is a critical (and perhaps obvious) starting point, and a whole book could be written about how to go about it, with chapter titles like "Know Your Audience for Who They Really Are," "Get Intimate," and "Be Ruthless about Setting Audience Priorities." I'll leave that work for someone else. For now, I have a few considerations for you to ponder as you walk through this initial step.

First, consider that, for most brands, there are generally three broad groups of people you should get to know: Saints, Sinners, and Undecideds.

Your saints love you above other brands in the same consideration set. They frequently buy you. They interact with you. They recommend you to others.

Love your saints. Embrace them. Talk to them. Regardless of what your brand sells, think of it as a service to your saints. Think about how you might extend that service to your mutual benefit. Give your saints tools and access so they can advocate for you. Overall, and as much as possible, your mode of communication with your saints should be two-way. If you can't do this in fact, find a way to do it in feeling.

As a consultant, I travel a lot, so I was a saint for United (Global Services) and American (Concierge Key). When I left Sterling Brands and took some time off, I was curious to see how these brands would respond to my lack of travel. American noticed immediately, and the communication stream began. It wasn't a particularly impressive effort, but it happened. United, however, didn't appear to notice. Keep in mind that "noticing" would take nothing more than a somewhat intelligent database query and an automatic communication program. Surely these are standard at this point? Also of note, United makes it incredibly hard to complain to them, even for their most loyal customers. And don't get me started on their noncompetitive in-flight program. Overall, they violate even a beginner's understanding of how to work with your saints. As I sit here sheltering in place, United is getting pummeled by the media because, unlike airlines that are taking social-distancing measures on their planes, United is filling every single seat, on fewer and smaller planes, for bicoastal travel. If there's some method to their madness, they certainly did not communicate it to their audience. Instead they let us derive our own conclusions. My conclusion? Their actions say, "To hell with customer safety, let's be as cost-efficient as possible." Who are these people?

To get to know your saints, I recommend an incredibly revealing exercise, something commonly known as a "customer journey map." First, no matter what you're selling, think of your business as a service. If it's a product, view that product as a service to your saints, and see where this perspective takes you. Next, map out the way your customers—saints first—walk through and interact with your brand. Look for the places you can initiate interaction. Look for strong points you might highlight to the benefit of the entire journey. Perhaps most importantly when it comes to your saints, look for the weak links in the chain that might cause someone to drop out.

Service your saints. Embrace your saints. It's really, really good for business.

As for your sinners? Ignore them. Do the research necessary to identify them, but only so that you can then avoid them. These people are exercising their right to have absolutely nothing to do with your brand. They will never buy what you're selling, so any thinking that includes them is tainted. Don't include them in any average you create when analyzing your business. Avoid them as completely as you can, as any money spent on them is completely wasted.

Set your sinners aside.

Then consider the undecideds. They're on the fence, and you need to pull them over to your side. Don't do one of those expensive mass-audience-segmentation studies that rarely lead to action— segment your undecideds and only your undecideds. Know your positioning strategy, define their segments, then consider how to translate your position for the most promising subsets.

When considering your undecideds, you need to be totally ruth-less about who qualifies as promising. In the good old days, a mar-keter might have defined a reachable undecided as anyone whose "intent to buy" was above five on a ten-point scale. In other words, if a prospect filling in a short survey indicated they "might" buy a product or service, they were considered reachable.

Today, "might" means "not."

Might is a hope. Might is ridiculously optimistic. Might ignores real life and the many noisy alternatives between you and that prospect. Today, a reachable undecided has to score eight or higher on that ten-point scale. The scale you use isn't the point here, just be brutally honest about your real-world chances of moving some-one who generally doesn't want to be moved.

So this idea of saints, sinners, and undecideds is something to consider.

A second consideration, mentioned earlier, is the observation that great brands target narrow and catch wide. Great brands don't try to be all things to all people; they try to be one thing to the peo-ple they care about most. Of course, if these people are aspirational to the rest of us, these brands will catch wide.

Positioning yourself to your audience, particularly in a business-to-business marketing context, is similar to a cocktail party. All of your audiences are in attendance, and you have to decide which one you will speak to directly. You do so secure in the knowledge that, when you speak, others will be listening in over your shoulder. As an example, Visa talks to consumers directly, but it knows its real customers are the banks. When we recommended a "better money" positioning strategy for the Visa brand, built on the benefits of plastic over paper, we did so in part because this message benefits Visa's bank customers, who make more money when we use credit cards than when we use paper. I would also argue that the message benefits card holders, so everyone at this particular cocktail party can win. Visa speaks to individual consumers, to the assumed benefit of their bank customers, who are intently listening in.

Note that no matter your target audience, other audiences will always listen in on your conversations, so you have to assume complete transparency. Even when you focus on one audience, assume that what you say to them will be heard by others. To illustrate, once upon a time, Norwegian Cruise Line wanted to appeal to a younger demographic. They introduced a new, award-winning ad campaign that showed a bunch of beautiful, scantily clad young people frolicking on a beach with their ship in the background. A couple of problems: young people didn't want to have anything to do with cruises, and older people, the real cruise customers, didn't want to have anything to do with a cruise that featured a bunch of young people partying on the beach. The campaign completely backfired and did significant damage to their business.

Another marketer, who sold ingredients to a wide range of branded consumer-product manufacturers, once ran a consumer campaign that claimed, essentially, "We're not the ones who make this; we're the ones who make it better." Of course, this marketer's customers saw the ad and it didn't go over well. You don't have to be a sophisticated marketer to know taking credit for your customer's products is probably not the best strategy available.

A third consideration: smart marketers go past traditional audience descriptions to build a very clear and detailed profile of what we might call their "design target." This is the person they want the world to believe their brand is built for, the person they want their organization to have in mind as they go about their jobs every day. The key: this person should be aspirational (but not out of reach) to the brand's core audience.

Nike does this really well. We know Nike's design target is a high-performing, extremely competitive athlete, someone looking for every possible winning edge. Importantly, this person is aspirational—the rest of us would like to think we've got a bit of this athlete inside us. While the reality is that the majority of Nike footwear is essentially worn to the grocery store, when we put those shoes on, we are assuming that badge, wearing it because we think it's a part of us, however small that part might actually be.

The Nike design target is clear, but is this the case with your business? When working with clients, one of our first checks concerns consistency of audience viewpoint. We ask a simple question of anyone who has customer contact: Can you paint me a picture of who your customer is? We usually get a wide range of answers rather than a consistent and tightly defined response. Part of the marketer's task is to create a very clear and consistent internal picture of the customer, so the organization knows who it is communicating with, at all times and in all ways. As you would expect, it's tough to communicate with someone effectively if you don't know exactly who they are.

This brings us to yet another know-your-audience consideration, critical marketing mass. Imagine a person facing an almost infinite line of Coke machines. They quickly walk down the line, placing $1.00 in each machine. By the time they finish, they've spent millions. There's only one catch—a Coke costs $1.25, so they've spent a lot of money and have absolutely nothing to show for it. I see this all the time: Marketers trying to do too much and spreading their resources too thin. Marketers trying to reach too many people and therefore effectively reaching nobody. To use yet another metaphor, too many marketers swim along, just under the surface. Because they are constantly swimming, they can go a long distance, but no one ever sees them. Instead, they need to gather their resources and leap out of the water as high as they can. They might have enough energy for only one leap, but being seen clearly once is infinitely better than gliding along unseen forever.

I discovered the importance of critical marketing mass early in my life, when running marketing and sales for Kellogg's Australia. Each year, like all packaged goods brand-management teams, we asked each brand manager to create a marketing plan for the following year. This was the biggest day on their calendar. Brand managers would look at their P&L, which yielded a general sense of marketing spend, then they would create the plan they thought made the most effective use of that budget. As head of marketing, I assessed and helped refine each brand plan, then off we went into planning for the coming year.

Eventually I realized this practice violated my idea of critical marketing mass, putting us in danger of doing a lot of things "pretty well." So I changed the approach. The plan development looked the same, but brand managers were told that we would extract all the tactical plans from each brand and then list them in order of the impact we felt each tactic would have in the market-place. Once we had agreed on our priorities, we assigned a "cost of success"—the budget we felt was really required for that tactic to grab the attention of a reluctant audience. We then took each tactic's budget, in order of perceived impact, and kept a running cumulative total. Working down our tactical priority list, as soon as we had used up the total company spend, we drew the line and stopped.

Two benefits resulted from this approach. First, we ensured critical marketing mass behind the most impactful tactics. Second, we did less, so our team could get a lot closer to executional perfection. While this may seem counterintuitive to some, doing less—with more critical mass and better execution—is definitely the way to go. Bottom line—we did less and got more, reversing a fifteen-year decline in market share and ultimately gaining all of that share back in only four years.

So, let's apply the same approach to your target audience. Prioritize your audience carefully, and ensure you reach your top-priority audience effectively before you spend even a penny against the next priority. If you can't build critical mass nationally, pick a region. If a region is still too large, pick a city. Philosophically, when a window is open, it's better to jump too far through it than to come up short. Going too far means you got through that window. Coming up short means you did not. Assume it's this binary and you'll be a much happier, not to mention more successful, marketer.

As a working strategist, I often speak to people who want to break the world of marketing strategy into two parts—businesses that target business audiences and businesses that target consumer audiences. I don't want to spend much time on this distinction, but I do want to make a couple of points before moving on.

The first point is that any marketer has to know their audience inside out. Who they are, how they think, their cultural context, and much more. This is a constant, regardless of who that audience happens to be. Once the audience is understood, the task is to position your "thing" in a way that delivers differentiated advantage—a second constant.

Yes, the nature of a business sell is different. The cost is often much higher; therefore the associated risk is much greater. Consideration generally lasts longer and is more deeply analytical. Relationships become a much greater part of the equation. I talked previously about building a "customer journey map," and want to stress that this skill can be dramatically more important in a business-to-business marketing model.

These selling mechanics and others cannot be ignored, but the task remains essentially the same: Know your audience and find your differentiated advantage. Build your marketing efforts around that difference and stay focused. I think that consumer marketers and those that sell to businesses can learn a lot from each other, blending more sophisticated consumer-insight tools with a more intimate form of customer understanding.

A much larger topic for someone else's book, but something worth thinking about.

I can't leave this topic without unloading three complaints about marketers and how they find their audience.

My first complaint is ageism. Regardless of their own age, marketers are chronic ageists. I will hear marketers talk about people in their fifties, with twenty to thirty years of very high spending ahead, as an audience that's "dying off." Money is money. A dollar in boomer revenue is the same as a dollar in millennial revenue. Yes, I know millennials have more years ahead of them, but do you really think your investment in them will create a lifetime of loyalty to your brand?

To illustrate, the average age of a television news viewer is around sixty-five, yet broadcasters routinely create "core audience profiles" using people in their forties. Essentially, they are embarrassed by the age of their audience. For years, Levi's pursued hip, young, urban guys, despite the fact that these guys had made it clear they wanted nothing to do with the brand. Worse, even if Levi's could turn that perception around, these guys wouldn't be caught dead in the retailers that carried Levi's. Meanwhile, back at the ranch, other brands were stealing Levi's real audience—the older, decidedly unhip American heartland. These people loved the Levi's brand, but it had gone missing as it focused its marketing efforts entirely on those it couldn't reach. While it's great to have aspiration for your brand, wishful thinking is dangerous.

The Boston Consulting Group projects that by 2030, the US fifty-five-plus population will have accounted for half of all domestic consumer-spending growth since the Great Recession, a number that rises to 67 percent in Japan and 86 percent in Germany. According to the US Bureau of Labor Statistics, in 2017, adults fifty-five and up accounted for 41 percent of annual consumer expenditure.

Most importantly, I'm not the only one who has noticed that marketers are ageist. Nearly eight out of ten US adults fifty and older feel they are being overlooked by advertisers, according to a recent study by the Video Advertising Bureau.

For some reason, millennials are the group marketers currently want to talk about. The group they want to pursue, whether their product or service suits this demographic or not. And what is a millennial? Some are forming families, while others are out at bars with their friends. Marketers talk about this group as if it were a real entity of some kind. Are they suggesting a millennial in Brooklyn has more in common with a millennial in rural Alabama than with an older consumer in Manhattan?

Let's not talk about generations as if they're a voting bloc. Always be wary of averages, and never, ever average across groups that are different along dimensions important to your business.

My second complaint is urban bias. Marketers live in big cities. They have college degrees and like to think of themselves as on trend and in the know. When most of them picture their audience, they imagine people they can understand—people a lot like them. As a result, they miss a whole "heartland mindset," even when these consumers make up the bulk of their business. Here's a really good tip—talk to Paul Jankowski and his team at New Heartland Group, based in Nashville, and have your eyes truly opened to this consumer. They might not be like you, but there are a lot of them,

and you will learn to love them. Even without the help of consultants, you can get to know this audience. Organize an expedition to
the wilds of small-town America. See what you learn. When I was
at Sterling Brands, one of our strategists adopted a small town in
the South, really getting to know the mayor, the school principal,
the bar owner, and many other locals. He then led some clients for
a visit—up close and personal. Try it. You won't be in Kansas any-
more, Dorothy. And that's a good thing.

My third complaint is the segmentation study. I was once
told by a client that only 50 percent of segmentation studies are
acted upon by the organization they are supposed to serve. These
are expensive, time-intensive, unwieldy instruments that benefit
the research companies that conduct them but—I would argue—
seldom benefit the people who pay for them. It's tough to argue
with research like this, as having more information is generally
considered a good thing. But what's the opportunity cost of spending time and money on studies that won't help you, as opposed to
spending it on something much more strategically actionable?

Way too often I run into people who believe that market-wide
segmentation can drive strategy, instead of the other way around.
The root of the problem is that in order to create attitudinal segments, you have to average across all the people you include in the
survey. When you do this kind of analysis, you're factoring in a lot of
the wrong people. In my mind it's strategy first, then a specific form
of segmentation based on that strategy. If you're set on a segmentation study, you must first define your positioning strategy and
your addressable audience. You are marketing an idea—how does
your intended audience segment based on their response to that
idea? You might separate the market into some form of our saints,
sinners, and undecideds, or might do something more specific to
your particular needs. However you do it, only once you understand your strategy and have some picture of your high-potential

audience should you segment them (and only them) into smaller, more exactly addressable segments.

You might call this strategically driven segmentation.

Let's use a movie sequel as a simple illustration. For every sequel, there are those who will never go to a cinema to watch it, those who are already mentally lining up to attend, and those who are thinking about it. Much of movie advertising is created for those who are going to attend anyway—our saints. Instead of creating a campaign that just the saints will love, what if you did a quick survey that identifies unique characteristics of the saints, sinners, and undecideds? What if you then spoke only to the undecideds to identify a few key subgroups and the positioning or framing approach that will best pull them over to your side of the fence? Perhaps some will be swayed by the romantic subplot, while others love the technology or psychological subplots. Without straying from the true overall position for the movie, you can then play up the specific dimensions, subplots, and characters that will bring in the undecideds without alienating the saints. Because you know who they are, you can also better focus your media spending on the undecideds and, just as importantly, away from the sinners.

End of complaining. On to our second step.

STEP 2: FIND YOUR DIFFERENCES.

Yes, this step is really as simple as it sounds: find your differences. At this stage in the search, be ruthlessly honest, but don't edit based on how meaningful the difference actually is (that will come later in the process). For now, just identify the differences. They can be functional, found in the product or service itself. They can be more emotional, found in the organizational or customer culture. But they need to be something that's as different as possible.

Before you start your search, here are a couple of cautionary notes. First, as mentioned earlier, remember that "better" is not different. By and large, "cheaper" is also not different. A while back I was asked to speak with the CEO of a startup in the apparel space. It looked like he had a really interesting way to position his brand against industry norms, not unlike the way Dove did in the beauty category. But all he wanted to talk about was price, repeatedly stating how much cheaper they were than the market leader. The truth was, pricing wasn't a significant category obstacle, and several competitors were already taking up the low end of the market. With a couple of fairly successful retailers called Amazon and Walmart to consider, "cheaper" just wasn't a viable long-term position to occupy. To cut a long story short, I failed miserably in my attempt to move him away from price toward a more uniquely category-disruptive strategy.

Please don't make the same mistake. Unless you have fundamentally reengineered your category, "cheaper" is not a sustainable differentiated advantage.

"Better" and "cheaper" are not differentiated advantages in their own right, but that doesn't mean they can't be fertile ground for growing difference. Unless you have created a business model that, from the ground up, is built to deliver a sustained advantage on price or quality, you're inevitably spending time and money on a difference that competitors can take away, if even for an equally fleeting moment in time. Walmart stands for everyday low prices. They simplify. They don't actually promise to be cheaper on every item, but they promise to be your best possible partner when it comes to your wallet. The shopper feels Walmart is doing everything possible to reduce costs and therefore keep those costs out of their shopping basket.

Similarly, there are cases where a profoundly important quality difference can yield differentiated advantage, especially when driven by a strong, compelling point of view. Apple. HBO. Emirates.

Four Seasons. When Lexus launched, they did an amazing job of reminding us that car badges were emotional BS; what people really needed was a high-quality car. If you were around at the time, you saw a campaign featuring one commercial that simply showed a ball bearing running smoothly along the incredibly tight seams between the body panels. The point? Lexus doesn't just look like it's put together well; it actually is. Lexus took the badge value out of the luxury-car equation and simply demonstrated that they'd made a better product. In an emotional, badge-driven category, this was a unique brand point of view, supported by a tangible product difference. This is the essential combination you're looking for.

Okay, one more cautionary note: be sure to separate hygiene factors from true differences. For example, if you work in media, in the early stages of your search for difference, someone is sure to list some version of "entertaining" as a difference. If customer service is important to your business, "service" will most certainly get an early mention. "Trust" is another frequent mention—differentiating only in a world where competitors position themselves as untrustworthy. In general, these are hygiene factors: they are incredibly important, and without them you will surely lose any competitive battle, but they are not differences unless there is something truly unique about them. Let me repeat this: your performance on hygiene factors can make or break your business, but generally speaking they are not productive positioning fodder unless there is something compellingly different about the way you actually do them.

Look at your business from different vantage points, as your most powerful differences might exist at the brand level, the product level, or even the feature level of the customer experience. At the brand level, the difference might be found in how your brand uniquely connects, or could connect, to the culture it seeks to serve. Or it may be that the most powerful difference sits with the overall product experience you've created. As we'll discuss later, the "catalyst" may even exist at the feature level, where a specific feature essentially brings to life a much larger difference that the brand can stand for. In searching up and down this architecture for the most powerful differences, always favor the tangible over the conceptual.

Though we see a lot of it—too much, in my opinion—these days, conceptual marketing feels like an artifact of a bygone age. Avoid it if at all possible. To illustrate, many years ago, in my advertising agency life, we were asked by Sony to develop a $100 million global brand campaign. We were an ad agency, so we dutifully set about following our instructions. But I argued that a brand-level campaign would prove way too conceptual. At the altitude at which the Sony brand operated, over all its products and services, the air was just too thin. My counterargument: we should codify the Sony brand values and then, each quarter, assign $25 million to the product that was the most compelling example of those values. This way the consumer would see a tangible expression of the Sony brand. They would see something compelling that they could actually buy. Internally, the product managers would compete for the $25 million bonus spending, and the most exciting and "on-brand" products would bring Sony to life in an immediate and relevant way. Each quarter would bring something new to the consumer. Everyone wins. Unfortunately (at least in my mind), I lost the argument and was told to get back on the brand train. The result? As I recall it, if you were watching really, really closely, you saw a Sony brand ad featuring a Fabergé egg rolling down a hill. It was roundly criticized and quickly pulled. I may have the visual wrong, but the point is right: the campaign was entirely conceptual—internally inspiring, maybe, but externally vague and entirely forgettable.

Many years have passed since the almost-simultaneous launch of Lexus and INFINITI, but a comparison of their approaches is highly instructive. INFINITI went conceptual, presenting a Zen-like, quiet, and luxurious face, suggesting quality and expense. The problem was that they offered no specifics, therefore implying they were just like other luxury brands. Where's the compelling difference? Lexus did the opposite: they showed tangible, beautifully designed, extremely close-up demonstrations of quality, and they de-positioned luxury brands by implying, "If you're a badge-driven poseur, go ahead and buy them. But if you actually care about quality, check out Lexus." In short, Lexus gave us a unique and tangible way to look at luxury cars. Lexus beat INFINITI in the launch war, and the brand benefitted for years to come.

When it comes to difference, conceptual is weak and tangible is strong.

STEP 3: WHICH DIFFERENCES MIGHT PROVE MOST COMPELLING TO YOUR AUDIENCE?

Now our process starts to get tougher. It's time to explore your list of differences with your audience in mind. Which is most compelling to them?

Here's where research may come in. Larger marketers have in-house research departments and healthy research budgets, but anyone can come up with some fun, quick, low-cost alternatives to test customer waters, even if their budgets are small. For instance, during my Kellogg's days we simply asked brand managers and assistants to spend some time in the cereal aisle of a nearby supermarket. First, they watched people shop their categories for a day. That alone can be educational. Second, we loaded them up with a few arguments—positioning ideas—we wanted to test on shoppers, plus some coupons of increasing value, and they headed back to the supermarket to try to convince a customer buying a directly competitive brand to buy the closest Kellogg's equivalent instead. In their first attempt, they could use only words to position the Kellogg's brand in a differentiated and, we hoped, compelling way. Failing that, they could use a coupon, gradually increasing the value until the purchase was free.

Real-world positioning research, for free. Try it sometime.

Keep in mind that, ultimately, your difference-based positioning strategy will be an internal asset. It will guide and inspire external expression, but it won't see the light of day. I see a lot of marketers test positioning statements with consumers, which is always a mistake. It's the idea that's important, not the poetry of the words used to convey it. Any difference you think may prove compelling is home to a range of hypotheses which, if proven, make that difference a valid candidate. Deconstruct your difference into the hypotheses that need to prove true if it is to be viable, then test those hypotheses—the thoughts, not the language.

When we were conducting research for MSNBC, I didn't care what words formed the MSNBC positioning statement—that's an internal asset. I needed to know how high-potential viewers felt about the idea: Would a liberal audience support a progressively positioned news channel? With the *TODAY* show, we needed to know if people saw *TODAY* as more news oriented and *GMA* as more entertainment oriented. Could news be the better badge? With Dove, we needed to know if women were pissed off about how the beauty category markets itself. Would they like hearing that beauty comes from within?

Additionally, positioning research has to be uniquely rigorous. If your audience likes a positioning idea, that's not enough. They must *love* it. Women said, "Hallelujah!" to the Dove difference, and liberals quite literally cried when they talked about the MSNBC position. If you get approval from someone, challenge that approval. Challenge their agreement with you. That's what will happen in real life. In real life, someone is going to challenge your audience's idea about your product. A friend or family member or competitor will say what you're selling is stupid, and your positioning idea has to survive that real-world challenge.

All the while, remember this: good marketers see customer research as helpful, but they do not see it as something that provides "the answer." There's a key difference between you and your audience—you care deeply about who wins a long-term, highly competitive battle; they don't care at all. You care deeply about finding a differentiated position; they couldn't care less. Use your customer research as invaluable input into a decision only you can make.

STEP 4: HOW CAN A COMPELLING DIFFERENCE FORM A COMPETITIVE ADVANTAGE?

Now the list of differences gets shorter and things get tougher still. Explore each difference that seems compelling, to see if there's a way to spin it to your unique competitive advantage. Don't kill anything before you've played with it to see how much competitive leverage it might contain. Spin it around and see if you can find any juice.

If you're struggling with finding competitive advantage, take a look at how your competitors are positioning themselves. Do some form of SWOT analysis (strengths, weaknesses, opportunities, and threats). Ask yourself: *If I forget Austin's insistent and annoying demand for absolute difference, how would I position myself just to mess up the efforts of my major competitors? If they are positioning on one idea, what's the idea that would de-position them?* Try it, see what you have on the whiteboard, then reapply steps 2 and 3 and see what happens.

Remember the JCPenney story? If I'm JCPenney and I look at competitors like Walmart and Target, I see strength that can be exploited in apparel. While both can sell apparel at low prices, neither of these highly successful retailers can afford to create a comfortable experience within which shoppers can find styles that actually fit. It just doesn't match their business model. It's harder—though not impossible—for online competition. In general, while fit is something that can be assumed at the high end of retail, that's not so at the low end. So fix up your fitting rooms, invest in same-day alterations, and make "fit" your differentiated advantage.

Similarly, if you want to position yourself against a search generalist, position as a search specialist. If YouTube is chaos, create a highly structured, intuitively navigated viewing experience. If Twitter can get ugly really fast, leave it to the trolls and create a much gentler environment within which people can share more peaceful observations and thoughts. If ice cream is all about a bewildering array of flavors, even though the big three dominate, become the master of vanilla. And so on . . .

Here are a few other questions to consider: Who is the competition that provides the greatest opportunity for differentiated advantage? For example, do you have permission to position yourself as the category leader, working against other competitive forces and categories on behalf of your audience, or are you competing within the category? Amazon could position itself against other online retailers, but where's the juice in that? They own over half of all online retail sales, so why not take on the act of physical shopping? Shoppers can get dressed, get in their car, drive, and hope to find (and pay for) a good parking spot, then hope to find what they want in their size, then drive home. Or they can stay in their slippers, go to Amazon, and find everything they need within minutes. This is just what you're looking for: a clear choice between boots and slippers. To me at least, this juxtaposition has tons of competitive advantage, lots of emotional drama, all of which would be lacking if Amazon identified their competitive set as a bunch of smaller, online retailers.

The act of defining your market can be critical. Years ago, *Harvard Business Review* published a great piece by Ted Levitt, "Marketing Myopia." Check it out. It's dated at this point, but it still clearly demonstrates how the way we define our business, and therefore our competition, can dramatically affect our trajectory.

Okay, now have you found competitive advantage? If you're fortunate, at this point in the process you have alternative-positioning ideas. You have multiple candidates, each of which is different, compelling, and competitively advantageous. If that's not possible, hopefully you have one powerful candidate that you're really excited about. But what if you don't? What if you are sitting in that room completely empty-handed?

First, close the door and sigh. It's okay. Let it out. If appropriate, pour yourself a drink. Wait, screw appropriateness, just pour yourself a drink. You have something to sell and you have found nothing unique about it, nothing that makes it different in any compelling way. You tried, and you failed. There you are, alone, drink in hand, facing reality: your baby has no differentiated advantage. Give yourself a moment to grieve. Then shake it off, because this is where the real fun starts: Now you get to make something up. Now you have an opportunity to flex your creative muscles and truly *create* difference.

First, look back at the process and be brutally honest about where it failed. Did you find differences but feel they wouldn't prove sufficiently compelling to your audience? Did you uncover compelling differences that don't really create competitive advantage? Where is the weak link in the chain? Sometimes you'll find little real difference at the product or brand level, but you can still find difference in the way your brand interacts with consumer, cultural, or category dynamics. It's a good idea to consider this in any circumstance, but especially if you're not impressed by the possible differentiated advantages that lie within your business.

Next, consider other brands that have created difference brilliantly. Brands like Dove, Corona, Halo Top, and Old Spice. Do their lessons apply? Like Apple AirPods, can you conjure up your parent brand in an incredibly compelling way? Like Jif, can you commit to working with your advertising agency to create a cinematic experience around a jar of peanut butter? Like Splenda, do you have the nerve to turn a misperceived product weakness completely on its head? In short, go to school with those who have truly created difference, and see what inspires you personally.

Then ask yourself a few specific questions. Is there a category-based opportunity to differentiate? Can you slice and dice the category to create a category of one? What is the emotional high ground of the category from a consumer perspective? Does a competitor already own it? If not, how can you own it? What category-related things are bugging customers, and how might your brand address them?

Yes, the "create difference" scenario is less than ideal from a business perspective, but for a marketer it can lead to an incredibly rewarding personal experience. Maybe you didn't invent this thing you're selling, but now you're creating its differentiating brand point of view. Sure, your difference would be stronger if anchored in the user experience, but it would be less heroic, right?

So if you can't find a compelling difference, don't despair. Finish your drink, sit down, roll up your sleeves (if you have them), and create one.

STEP 5: ASK YOURSELF A FEW
QUESTIONS AS YOU PROCEED.

Okay, let's say you've narrowed down your options. You've found or created a differentiated position that you'd call compelling. Now run it through a four-point test.

Is it culturally noisy? While "different" and "disruptive" can be mutually supportive, they are also separate considerations. Think of your marketing strategy as a box. When it comes to positioning strategy, *don't think outside the box*. It's easy to be attracted by that highly creative space that sits outside the strategy. It's tempting, but it's off-strategy and intellectually lazy. Don't go there.

That said, it's also self-defeating to create a positioning strategy that sits quietly in the middle of the box. Here you might find an intellectually appropriate positioning solution, but it won't be sufficiently different or compelling. In other words, it will be on-strategy but culturally quiet. You'll never be criticized for it, but you'll never get famous either.

The culturally noisy positioning solution sits close to the box's inside edge. It stretches and challenges the limits of your strategy. This positioning solution is both different and compelling to the marketplace. In fact, the edges of your strategy box are the only places from which you can create relevant noise. You just need to find them and start banging.

The best marketers intuitively understand this, because the best marketers have high DQ. Without naming names, I've been lucky enough to work with a long list of great marketers. These people realize that they must do something unique, strategically and tactically, if they are going to win for the businesses they serve. You don't need to sell them difference; you need to help them find it. On the other hand, I've also worked with equally smart people with low DQ. These people approach marketing purely analytically, looking for the intellectually correct answer. Both high-DQ and low-DQ people understand the need for a strategic box, but one group is determined to make noise at the edges, while the other is content to sit quietly in the middle. I worked with a low-DQ marketer recently who felt his job was simply to find that intellectually correct answer, then hand it to those crazy, creative agency types to work with. Not fair to the agency, and not fair to the company he works for.

Put your differentiated strategy through a cultural-noise stress test. Does it contain a high level of "creative energy"? Do marketing communications people get excited because they can quickly see the possibilities? Could you write a white paper on the point of view that sits behind your differentiated advantage? What would a positioning T-shirt say, and would you wear it?

All marketers have their favorite examples of noisy tactics. I've already mentioned many of mine, with more to come. I'm sure you have yours. Note that the best examples started from a difference-based position, which dramatically increased the chances of creating highly differentiated tactics. When a position has difference and cultural momentum, the tactical team's job is just so much easier, not to mention more rewarding and fun.

Is it simple and tangible? In case this wasn't already clear, I have an issue with conceptual marketing. I think its day, if it ever existed, passed long ago. A recent post on Markets Insider discussed the issues faced by 2019's slate of "unicorn" startups (those valued at $1 billion-plus). In brief, they identify three problems that would contribute to a significant valuation drop after going public. Not surprisingly, two of these problems were more financial in nature, but the third was titled "branding." Here are three of the "brand positions" featured in the article:

- WeWork's goal was "to elevate the world's consciousness."
- Peloton "sells happiness," according to its filing, "but of course, we do so much more."
- Lyft positions itself "at the forefront of a massive societal change."

Is this some form of jointly conceived prank? In their struggle to gain altitude, all three brand positions became remarkably vague. None relate to the business at hand. None are ownable in any way, shape, or form. It's great to have lofty ambitions, but how about actually telling me what you uniquely do? How about something tangible I can actually grab hold of? WeWork's stated purpose, even if it were the least bit honest, has absolutely zero relationship to what WeWork offers. As for Lyft, don't they understand they're number two? How about a purpose that shows me they are at least somewhat in touch with that reality? Peloton sells happiness, which is only different if everyone else is selling sadness. Not to mention, when anyone adds "we do so much more," they are indicating a lack of internal focus. Did someone important in the room want to ensure they could extend their brand into anything and everything?

Generally, customers couldn't care less about grand concepts, or who wins and who loses. They're just not that interested. Meanwhile, marketers are probably way *too* interested in these things. Try pulling yourself away from your business and viewing it all through dull glasses. Assume no one cares about your efforts but you. Now find something that real people with busy lives might actually care about, and make some noise with it.

Customers don't deal well with concepts, not because they're dumb, but because real people lead busy, fully occupied lives. Give them something tangible to hang on to. Something to do. Something easy to share and talk about. Something real. If that "tangible" requirement can't be filled at the brand level, find or create a brand "catalyst." Ask yourself: What is the tangible product, service, or even feature that can prove most catalytic to the position you want to occupy? In other words, what real thing best brings the position to life for your audience? If you have a good answer, consider focusing your entire marketing effort on that tangible catalyst—it may be exactly the door opener you need.

My favorite illustration of this point is really dated, but it's also really useful. In the early days of this thing we call the internet, Sun Microsystems was a leading server company. They developed a programming language called Java, designed to write once and run anywhere—perfectly suited to internet-based application. Led by a very smart, creative product manager named Kim Polese, Sun marketed Java in a light, approachable manner—not at all what you'd expect from a large server company. They focused their marketing effort on the language itself, saying, essentially, "If you want to use the internet to your business advantage, you need to talk to us about this language." Desperate to have this conversation, businesses flocked to Sun. Invariably, they talked about Java, then left the building with a bunch of Sun servers to run it. In other words, Sun recognized that Java was their catalytic product. A real, tangible product that positioned them as an internet thought leader, selling a ton of servers along the way.

Of note, the catalytic product need not be a huge business contributor. Java represented a couple of percentage points of Sun's revenue, but it opened the door to the remaining 98 percent.

I previously mentioned Best Buy using service as a differentiated advantage over Amazon. Their catalytic product was the Geek Squad, and bringing this powerful resource to life should continue to be central to their positioning strategy.

The iPod was an incredibly catalytic product for Apple, as was the iPhone, then the App Store. When Apple communicates with us, note that they do so through real, often relatively small and specific, catalytic features, not some broad conceptual sell.

The Escalade was a catalytic product for Cadillac, completely changing the way we saw this brand. Oldsmobile told you they were "not your father's Oldsmobile" and failed. Cadillac didn't seek to convince you they'd changed; they simply showed you the car that proved it.

A range of incredible programs, most recently *Game of Thrones*, have been catalytic to HBO, while Netflix deftly hides its dogs and uses its stars as powerful brand catalysts.

Maps are catalytic to Google. They don't make money, but they keep us bound to the brand and appreciative of its service, day in and day out. There's nothing more emotionally bonding than having someone guide you when you're lost.

That's what I mean by tangible.

Is it sustainable? Lastly, you need to consider sustainability, but not in the way you might think. When testing for sustainability, most people ask if their differentiated advantage will stand the test of time and competitive pressure. If you are looking at two strong positioning candidates, this might be considered a good tiebreaker, but I think that level of sustainability is becoming less important. In today's market, we have to consider the "disposable strategy." In a technology-enabled and highly cluttered competitive environment, strong moves are more easily and quickly matched. Given this environment, a really strong difference with a shorter expected shelf life will have greater impact than a weak but totally sustainable difference.

Don't walk away from a strong positioning move because you think it might not hold up over time. Instead build a road map, plotting out how you will evolve the strategy over time. Spend some time properly war-gaming competitive responses and potential marketplace shifts. Don't just do the normal competitive analysis, but actually become the competition and build a full-frontal assault on your proposed position. What would you do if you were them? Build their attack, then build your defense. That defense will consist of proactive tactical changes and prepared reactions should certain attacks materialize. In other words, a bit of planning ahead can make any positioning strategy more sustainable, while significantly reducing your reaction time to marketplace pressures and changes. The real trick is to know when you're creating something that must evolve, and to plan accordingly.

JUST FOR FUN, TRY APPLYING THESE STEPS TO THE BRAND THAT IS YOU.

While I readily admit that all this "personal brand" stuff irritates me, it's a useful exercise to apply this differentiated positioning process to your career.

Let's first remind ourselves of an obvious but often overlooked fact: each of us is an *n* of one. As Tyrion Lannister says in *Game of Thrones*: "Never forget what you are, for surely the world will not. Make it your strength. Then it can never be your weakness."

Business, like life, seeks to categorize us—by department, by skill set, by performance, even by attitude. Some companies have gone as far as to have people place their Myers-Briggs (a popular personality test) profile on their desks so that colleagues know how to best interact with them. While I find some of these classification techniques weird, I understand that categorization is useful, perhaps even necessary, when you have to organize large groups of people. So, fine, you'll be categorized. Welcome to the world of business. Institutions and large companies—perhaps the world around us—will seek to round off our edges. They've come to believe it's in their self-interest to do so.

But while "alike" works for efficiency, it doesn't work for effectiveness. I suspect the most effective companies have figured out how to harness difference. Consciously or unconsciously, formally or informally, they are encouraging and therefore harnessing the power of the individual. Perhaps this is what I appreciate most about Silicon Valley and technology. A group of extremely bright, nonconforming people have found a home that previously didn't exist. I have an amazing friend who's a self-confessed *Star Wars*–loving nerd. At work he always wears one of his collection of T-shirts, usually fresh, that proudly declares his full-nerd status. He's a Pakistan-born engineer who can understand almost any problem. He also happens to be a loyal, successful employee, because his company stays focused on how he thinks and the results he creates, rather than how well he fits the superficial success profile used by others.

Yes, mistakes happen in Silicon Valley, probably with a higher frequency than they do in "corporate America," but so do miracles. A whole group of incredibly bright individuals, otherwise destined to work in seldom-visited back rooms, are playing important, high-profile roles in companies that are shaping our future. How cool is that?

But what does all this have to do with you? Although one of my favorite quotes is attributed to a wide range of people, I'll continue to insist it was Oscar Wilde who said, "Be yourself, everyone else is taken." In other words, like my engineer friend, you have uniquely identifying strengths to bring to the table (or desk). If you cover up those strengths in order to fit in, you'll never bring your full potential to work. Instead, allow your powerful difference to come through. You owe it to yourself, and you owe it to the organization you work for. When a square peg keeps trying to fit into a round hole, there's a really good chance that the peg will break. Don't let this happen to you.

Advice is easy, and being your genuine self can be hard, but it really is the only way to truly succeed. As Thomas J. Watson, legendary CEO of IBM, once said, "If you stand up and be counted, from time to time you may get yourself knocked down. But remember this: Someone flattened by an opponent can get up again. Someone flattened by conformity stays down for good."

With this as context, let's see how you can apply some of those difference-based marketing steps to create a difference-based career.

First, know the table stakes and make sure you have them covered. Every company has its "table stakes" qualities, and without them you're a nonstarter. These characteristics won't uniquely identify you among the crowd, but without them you'll be looking for another job. As a young assistant brand manager fresh out of business school, I knew attention to detail was a critical table stake. I also knew it was a personal weakness. Though I felt its importance would decline as I rose through the ranks, I knew I had to hide this weakness to succeed in the early days of my career. It took some effort, but I did a reasonable job of the detail work, and I survived to the point where I could create work-arounds so this weakness wouldn't hold me back.

Some table stakes will be more important than others, but know them all and ensure you at least meet expectations.

Now, identify your difference. What unique ability would you like to be known for? What's the idea you want your organization to most readily associate with your name? How is this ability an advantage over the competition? How is it compelling to your audience—those whom you must impress in order to move up?

Okay, you've got your unique skill. Now, how can you bring this skill to life in the most effective way possible? Where is your differentiated advantage best applied? Given this difference, what is your catalytic application?

In short, and most importantly, be your unique self. Don't back away from your difference; embrace it. Figure out how to make the absolute most of it. Work for people who want you to apply your unique self to their problems and opportunities. Cover the table stakes, yes, but also be the person only you can be. Your difference is your path to personal success. Being true to it will make your career (and your life) so much more rewarding.

"We are all equal in the fact that we are all different. We are all the same in the fact that we will never be the same."
—C. JoyBell C.

CHAPTER 9

TEN THINGS TO CONSIDER AS YOU PURSUE DIFFERENCE

"When the winds of change blow, some people build walls and others build windmills."
—Ancient Chinese Proverb

Everyone has a spare parts box—the place you put the leftover nuts and bolts after you've finished your project, hoping they'll be useful somewhere else someday. Well, that's what you'll find here: a collection of common-sense advice and useful ideas meant to reinforce the importance of difference and provoke some new thinking. Let's get started.

1. LOVE ME OR HATE ME, JUST DON'T LIKE ME.

After an American Olympian took second place, Nike founder Phil Knight famously said, "He didn't win the silver; he lost the gold."

Polarizing? You bet. Clear positioning? Hell yes. Nike prides itself on unabashed competitiveness. Winning edge. If you can't take the heat, get off the court. This kind of corporate culture isn't for everyone, which is exactly the point. You know exactly where Nike stands, and you line up with them or against them. That's the way they want it.

That's the differentiated edge: love me or hate me, just don't like me.

Difference is not for the faint of heart. At its most powerful, difference is highly polarizing. You may need to steel yourself against the blowback.

Positioning is the art of sacrifice. What you don't do and what you're willing to give up are often more important than what you do and keep. The better you are at creating clear and meaningful difference, the more likely you are to find a group of people who really don't like what you're doing. That's okay.

An extreme example: AND1 once said about their brand name, "If you don't know what it means, we don't want you wearing our shoes." Got it.

Donald Trump is nothing if not polarizing. Yes, he lost the 2020 election, but 74 million Americans voted for him. While many were simply voting their party ticket, many millions consider him their champion. Along somewhat similar lines, America's news media has, deliberately in most cases, become highly polarizing. With the possible exception of the seemingly universally loved Dwayne "The Rock" Johnson, most celebrities have as many detractors as they do supporters. McDonald's is huge and successful, but it's hated almost as much as it is loved (33 percent of Americans love it, while 29 percent hate it). Another success story, Starbucks, is loved by 30 percent of us and hated by 23 percent.

As Alexander Hamilton (among many others) is thought to have said, "If you don't stand for something, you'll fall for anything." Except in marketing it's more like "If you don't stand for something, you'll fade into the background." Sure, you can try to stay safe, try not to offend, try to get everyone to like you, but you'll never forge that unique, powerful bond with people who could love you.

"Like" is a dull existence for people, and a weak existence for brands.

If you want people to love you, you've got to put your uniqueness out front and accept that other people just won't like you at all. Possibly people you actually work with. When your company is clamoring for new customers and more business, it takes nerve to deliberately ignore people your organization will inevitably want you to consider as prospects.

Earlier I mentioned the huge success of the Axe brand. Axe is owned by Unilever, who deserve a CPG bravery award of some kind for nurturing brands like Axe, Dove, and Ben & Jerry's. Axe succeeded by positioning itself as a brand by aggressive young men, for aggressive young men. I'm sure many people were offended by Axe advertising, both out in the marketplace and within Unilever. The pressure to compromise must have been ever present, but the brand stayed the course. Axe took no prisoners and made no apologies.

Apple has always had its lovers and its haters, and the ratio of the two has essentially defined its trajectory. Once upon a time, Apple lovers were a much smaller but more intensely loyal group. Now they are exponentially bigger, with a less intense but still palpable level of brand love. Apple's sheer size has dulled the passion of its followers a bit, but the brand has done an amazing job of maintaining its difference while building its relevance.

Then there's Las Vegas—a study in how not to differentiate, followed by an even better study in how to get it right. Many years ago, the Las Vegas brain trust became a bit delusional. They decided that Las Vegas had "grown up" and was ready to present itself as a family entertainment center. They were moderately successful in this endeavor—the city offers lots of entertainment options for kids—but ultimately they woke up and realized their profit margin is found in adult activities. They were right to see the potential of great hotels, themed experiences, and fine dining; they were wrong to think that these developments heralded a change in their brand.

Fast-forward a few years, and a new campaign appears: "What Happens in Vegas, Stays in Vegas." This new riff on an old line absolutely nailed the essence of the Las Vegas brand. Vegas is for adults. Yes, it is now a much more sophisticated product than it was, but its brand position remains the same. The lesson? Be true to who you are. Constantly evolve and improve the quality of your product, but be true to your brand and let the product work for you. If you were outraged by the Las Vegas campaign (which you might well have been), that's okay. By definition, you're not their audience.

The upshot: To polarize is good. To travel down the middle is bad. It's tempting, but it's unequivocally bad. Like people, brands are partly defined by the company they keep. By extension, they're also defined by the company they don't keep.

2. NICHE IS NOT A FOUR-LETTER WORD.

Niche is most certainly not a four-letter word, yet in many business circles it's treated as one. Perhaps the most egregious mistakes were made in the late '90s in the technology arena, as "niche" became a curse you placed on an idea you wanted to kill or a competitor you wanted to insult. The attitude of the day was that niche companies weren't going to make it. Niche startups weren't going to get that much-needed venture capital.

At that point in time, the key VC question for any startup was "What's the addressable market?" This is a dangerously naïve question, driven by number crunchers with zero understanding of strategy. I once had a VC patiently explain to me that they wouldn't back ideas without an addressable market of $1 billion-plus. Let's think about that. Facebook was designed for a school campus. Amazon just wanted to sell books. LinkedIn was a small networking product for businesspeople.

You get the drift.

Niche phobia caused companies with great, focused ideas to dilute them into generalist ideas that seemed to "address" a very large market. Trying to stand for too much, they stood for nothing.

But niche brands can be highly differentiated. These brands understand the axiom "Position narrow, catch wide." Build a fervent but limited following first, own a segment, and enjoy the higher margins that generally accrue to the smart niche marketer.

Here I want to break with "Position narrow, catch wide" and stress (maybe scream) that a highly profitable niche is not a bad place to stay.

Yes, it's true, businesses are like sharks—if they don't keep moving forward they will die. But moving forward and getting "big" are two very different ideas. To me, niche indicates focus, and focus is the friend of difference. Claim your niche. Stay focused until you really come to own it. Then think about how that niche can be expanded, how the idea the niche represents can be made bigger. Sometimes thinking small is actually the best and most unique way to think big.

Focus can be a hard sell if you're a strategy consultant. From my perspective, businesses are far too quick to spread their attention across more products or categories. These products and markets appear so tempting, and the numbers will look great on a piece of paper, but the real-world opportunity cost can be very high. Before you make a move like this, be sure you've really explored the full upside of whatever business you've been focused on up to that point in time.

My colleagues are generally tired of hearing this story, but this book gives me a new audience, so let me tell you about a focus-based decision that will always stay with me. When I was with Kellogg's, we re-entered the New Zealand market, selling through a very large food broker. Working with this broker gave us access to more than one hundred salespeople, so our market coverage would be complete.

But sales were slow to build. We came to realize that we weren't really getting the attention we needed from all those salespeople. So we replaced one hundred-plus shared salespeople with one single, solitary Kellogg's salesperson. You guessed it, sales took off.

To the broker sales team we were just another marketer on a list. If they encountered an obstacle of any kind, instead of fighting through it, they could simply move on to the next item to make an easier sale. Our single salesperson could only sell one thing—Kellogg's cereal.

The power of focus.

Earlier I mentioned my love for Allbirds shoes, a niche brand with a pretty intense following. All wool, these shoes are ridiculously comfortable. The company is niche only in the sense that they have a tiny share of a huge $86 billion US and $210 billion global shoe market. So, what does someone senior at Allbirds decide they should do? Get into athletic performance shoes and apparel.

I love your shoes, but what are you thinking? I love your shoes because they're comfortable, but your running shoes aren't as comfortable and I can't take them seriously as performance shoes. Apparel—are you kidding me? To be clear, if there was no such thing as opportunity cost, perhaps I'd change my point of view. I have no idea how much they're spending, but I've been inundated with their apparel advertising lately—all money that should have gone toward building their shoe business.

And where did the difference disappear to, as Allbirds moved from a unique all-wool, comfortable, washable shoe to clothing without a notable point of difference?

In 2019, Allbirds had sales of $100 million, or 0.1 percent of the US shoe market. Another 0.1 percent and they'll double in size. The world doesn't need another Nike, nor does it need another diversified footwear and apparel company. Apologies if this embarrasses you, but you make amazing shoes. Stay focused. To make up for any embarrassment caused, here's some free advertising: Buy Allbirds shoes, people—you'll love them!

I write this while sheltering in place in our home in Bodega Bay, a small fishing town north of San Francisco. In thinking through this question of focus, I'm reminded of a small local-food outlet that sells only clam chowder. You can have red or white, but it's clam chowder or nothing. Come weekends and tourism, the longest lines in the area—by far—are found at this tiny, counter-service-only establishment. Why? If you're a local, you know that a couple of larger, full-service restaurants have won the annual "best clam chowder" award. But those restaurants don't have long lines outside every weekend. They will never become as famous for clam chowder, simply because they'll never focus on clam chowder. Surely in the mind of the visitor, the one place that focuses entirely on clam chowder is the one place to go. Intellectually this makes sense. Emotionally it is a truth.

Stay focused. Stay different. Grow not through diversification, but through focus and difference.

Yes, at some point your area of focus may get close to a theoretical ceiling, but most companies diversify way too early. This early diversification is motivated by a limited view of a marketplace. For example, I worked with a food brand whose leaders, seeing an almost 70 percent category share, understandably believed they were close to a ceiling. But then we roughly calculated the number of meals eaten in America versus the number of occasions their category and brand were consumed. The total category had less than a 5 percent share of meal occasions.

As mentioned earlier, ESPN is either a dominant sports broadcasting brand or a sports-based entertainment brand with a lot of upside. Coke has enjoyed a dominant soft-drink market share, but once set a visionary goal of "a Coke within arm's reach of everyone."

The point is that ceiling height is entirely a matter of perspective. Before you even consider diversification, look at your area of focus from every possible angle. It's highly likely that growing while maintaining focus (and therefore difference) will be a much more profitable path forward.

Lately someone started calling businesses with huge scale but no apparent path to profitability "unicorns." Uber is a classic example, as was WeWork before we all saw through the con. Generally speaking, these companies created huge topline-revenue stories regardless of cost.

This makes sense in certain circumstances—where network effects and scale are essential to future success, and getting there first is the difference between that success and failure. This was certainly true in the early days of eBay, and Uber can easily justify such a claim. But surely even in these cases, there must be a recognized path to profitability. If I create a useful product or service, then give it away, I can get to scale pretty fast. But what will happen when I start charging the price I need to be profitable? You have to be absolutely confident in the answer to this question, or very persuasive when talking to investors.

While the history of Amazon might suggest otherwise, financial markets will—sooner or later—demand bottom-line performance as well as top-line growth.

Just before Google went public it had no clear path to profitability, but they created AdWords in the nick of time and the rest is history. As a counterpoint to Google, Facebook's business model fascinates me. Facebook created this incredible platform that we made our own. Our presence on Facebook feels like our personal property. For so many of us, it's the center of our digital lives. That is why Facebook took off, reached escape velocity, and successfully climbed into orbit. So far, so good. But I see a catch here. A tension. In order to make money, Facebook essentially has to invade our personal space to serve up things that commercial enterprises want us to see, based on a possibly invasive view of our lives.

Google invades our search behavior, much of which is commercial anyway, so the trade-off seems much more comfortable to me. Facebook invades our personal space—they're a commercial entity and have to do so in order to make money. I get it, but this tension will be a crucial, persistent, and tough-to-get-right issue for the Facebook team. Personally, I think they do a pretty good job of managing this tension. I also think we ask too much of them. Facebook is the world, presented digitally. Surely we can't expect Facebook to rid the world of all its ills?

Let's get back to my larger point. Scale is great, but owning a unique and highly profitable niche is also an accomplishment to be celebrated. Yes, if you can expand that niche without diluting the clarity of your position, have at it. Just don't consider it a necessary evolutionary step to move out of that niche and compete more broadly. Keep in mind that several focused and successful niche plays may well be a better path to higher revenue, higher margins, and less risk exposure than one big, broad play.

I thoroughly enjoyed working closely with Silicon Graphics (SGI) as they built the market for visual computing in the early '90s. But as a marketer without a lot of technology experience at the time, I was perplexed about why the term *niche* took so much abuse within the company. Instead of celebrating their high-end visual niche (with the highest hardware margins in the business), SGI caught scale fever. They believed they had to double in size. Great ideas were cursed with the response "That's too niche." They were convinced they had to spread their technology advantage across lower-priced, less mission-critical market segments. Then they decided to buy Cray, who made supercomputers so powerful and so limited in terms of customers that they were already being driven out of business by—wait for it—Silicon Graphics. Why? To get bigger, of course. To avoid being a "niche player." Perhaps SGI's downfall was inevitable, but I'll continue to wonder. If they'd stuck to their guns and celebrated the niche they owned instead of moving more mainstream, the outcome could have been very different.

Large packaged-goods companies also seem to pursue a sort of "anti-niche" strategy. Each year several entrepreneurial startups create niche products that, either slowly or very quickly, build a loyal and passionate following. Once they get to be "big enough," they are acquired by a much larger packaged-goods company that also operates in the category, usually for a lot of money. If that very same idea had been created within the larger acquiring company, it would have been deemed too small—too niche—to warrant the investment necessary to take it to market. Somewhat ironically, acquiring companies don't have the passion and patience required to build a niche brand, but they do seem to have the money to buy one once it's a success.

Pixar is a niche player, and that niche is very tightly defined. They make animated films that target children. Yes, they do this cleverly so that parents look forward to taking their kids, but that's their singular focus: make animated movies for kids. Oh, almost forgot, these films are amazing and award winning, and almost all of them make more than $500 million in revenue. Disney acquired Pixar, but instead of extending Pixar in ways that would dilute it, they essentially left it alone and let it play a catalytic role across all of Disney animation.

In summary, there's nothing wrong with truly excelling at one thing, and sometimes thinking small is the best path to becoming big. If something has to be a four-letter word, I'd argue that "big" is closer than "niche."

3. OWN SOMETHING.

Here's the goal: don't be a category player; be an owner. As possible, define a category in a way that positions you as a leader. Make yourself famous for something.

Put another way, don't get in the long line; create a line of your own. Allow me to both illustrate and digress, using a more tactical example. I worked with a United Nations–created organization called the Global Fund, whose mission was to eradicate AIDS, malaria, and tuberculosis around the world. I could talk about this organization for a long time, but for current purposes I'll focus on their desire to bring in corporate contributions to support their work. They envisioned asking each company for a few hundred thousand dollars, but I argued that this was the "long line." A ton of organizations were waiting in line for this scale of support.

The scope of the fight faced by the Global Fund was unimaginably huge. By dint of their creation, they actually had the ability to place Kofi Annan and Bill Clinton in a room to pitch a corporate CEO. My argument was this: "Ask for $25 million, directly from the CEO, and you'll be the only one in that line." We compiled a list of companies that could write this kind of check and that did business in the areas most affected by these diseases, then introduced the Global Fund to the CEO of one of these companies. Within weeks they had their first $25 million commitment.

This was an exercise in common sense, but also one of difference, which can be just as important tactically as it is strategically. In life, business, and marketing, "Find the short line" is a pretty good mantra. An even better mantra is "Create your own line."

Okay, enough of tactics. Let's talk strategy. This may be a blinding glimpse of the obvious, but you've got to do everything you possibly can to "own" something. In technology we talk about "space." In packaged goods we're "segmenting" like crazy—all toward the ultimate goal of finding, and laying claim to, an area that is valued by your audience.

Be first to own a category, a segment, a concept. If someone beat you to it, how can you reinvent the category (hopefully in a way that sidelines any previous ownership)? Can you segment the category and own a new and compelling idea as a result? In technology I like to compare the marketplace—with all of its analysts and influencers, competition and coopetition—to one massive, confusing conversation. What is your part of that conversation? In which area will you be a thought leader and therefore carry the loudest voice? Find it and own it, even if it's a relatively small part of the overall conversation. Become the go-to expert on a specific subject. Make sure analysts and the press always call you first for a point of view on this part of the conversation. Then figure out how your slice of the conversation can be moved closer to center stage.

On a scale that was possible only in the retail landscape of the past, this is what the so-called category killers—The Home Depot, Circuit City, and others—did to mass merchants such as Sears and Montgomery Ward. Victoria's Secret decided to carve out an ownership position in women's lingerie. Whole Foods took ownership of organic food retailing, using it to sell a lot of products that were less than organic. Intuit owns the idea of financial software. Netflix owns streaming entertainment, even though we may divide our streaming screen time. Apple owns smartphones, even though many of us use Android. Google owns search, YouTube owns creator-driven video, and so on.

What's next? I keep waiting for the emergence of online search "category killers" to lay claim to specialized applications of search technology. For the life of me, I can't understand why Yahoo! and then Microsoft decided to compete with Google across a broad search front. A frontal assault was bound to lose. A flanking assault at least had a shot. Create a brand that owns a specific area of search, then create another. Perhaps the closest thing to an example of this is WebMD, which had a great opportunity to own the idea of "health search." They haven't quite done so, but maybe it's not too late. I always thought Consumer Reports had an opportunity to own a very large search vertical, but they continue to sit on the periphery for most people. Kelley Blue Book and others are fighting it out in the automotive vertical. How else might someone come to segment and own a piece of our constant searches?

In some ways, this becomes a revealing test for a category leader. If a consumer needs category-specific information, do they immediately default to Google, or do they come to you? What percentage of category-specific (and remember, you get to define the "category") search behavior goes through the brand leader? As that leader, what could you do to own search behavior that is specific to the category you lead? Are you willing to concede category search to Google? While it may not be worth the effort to compete on search for your category, at least explore the question.

For example, if I'm Disney and I license an incredibly wide range of consumer products based on characters my company created, am I comfortable with people using Google to find them? Whenever they do, I have consciously ceded control of the process to them. What if this lowers the price consumers pay? What if the resulting retail experience sucks? What if a paid ad for a Minion or a Warner Bros. character catches the searcher's eye and pulls them away from the Disney product they were looking for originally? In other words, should Disney have an amazing search engine, completely dedicated to finding all things Disney through a Disney-caliber consumer experience? Maybe so. Maybe not.

This search challenge represents a missed opportunity for TV Guide and WebMD. The hotel business can only bemoan the fact that their category search is dominated by others such as Google, Tripadvisor, and Expedia. Are OpenTable and Rotten Tomatoes making the most of their categories? Shouldn't ESPN own search for the sports category? Regardless of the answer, it's a fascinating question to explore (a fascinating question with big financial implications).

Speaking of OpenTable, what is wrong with this brand? It feels as if this icon has just been sitting there on my phone, doing nothing to improve or broaden its relationship with me. Worse, it feels as if the same is true for restaurants. For example, restaurants are going through the worst period of time in history, yet as far as I know, OpenTable has proceeded as if nothing has happened. Why is there no "pay forward" ability, so we loyal and passionate customers can give our favorite restaurant owners money now for a meal when it's safer? A restaurant gift certificate, if you will. It would take OpenTable a day to set this up on their site and get some form of insurance to cover any restaurant closures. Come on, people, how about doing something good for the community you're supposed to support?

Apologies for yet another digression, and back to our broader questions: How are you genuinely unique? What can you be the best at? Can this strength be applied to a specific market segment? Can you own something?

In building a brand and business, owning will always beat renting. So take your business apart and, with a cold, objective eye, find the one thing you can and must own, then find a way to stake your claim.

4. ECCENTRICITY RULES.

The idea of doing something truly different is so alien to some people that no amount of "proof" will coax them into taking the leap. But lately I've been wondering if "difference" is a bar set high enough. Maybe we need something stronger than differentiation? Something more extreme? Something eccentric?

I aspire to eccentricity, but I'll never get there, so I'm a bit jealous of true eccentrics. They follow their own path, frequently surprise us with their unique takes on things, and generally stand out from our day-to-day expectations. Whereas most people in business settings are fairly predictable, you never quite know what's going on inside an eccentric mind. While I care more than I probably should about what other people think, these folks don't seem to notice. They're not callous or antagonistic; they're just doing their thing. Sometimes they get it really wrong, and sometimes they get it so very right. Either way, they add a jolt of color to an otherwise gray business day.

Many of our favorite brands were built by determined and eccentric entrepreneurs. Mark Zuckerberg and Facebook. Oprah Winfrey and Harpo. Richard Branson and Virgin. Herb Kelleher and Southwest. Phil Knight and Nike. Jeff Bezos and Amazon. Sergey Brin and Larry Page and Google. Steve Jobs and Apple (and Pixar). Sam Walton and Walmart. Jake Burton and Burton Snowboards. Ben and Jerry and their ice cream movement.

I'm curious, would their friends and relatives say these icons always stood out, or would they say that success itself created that eccentricity? I'm betting it's a bit of both: these were unique, somewhat eccentric figures for whom incredible success acted as permission to let their freak flags fly.

These people aren't just eccentrics, they're leaders. Not necessarily the best managers, but true leaders. Their empires were born out of a strong and heartfelt point of view. The teams they built shared a real passion for what they were creating. As a group, they shared a mission. As customers, we picked up on this mission and joined the movement. We felt a sense of ownership, a sense of responsibility for their success, and we happily urged our friends to join us.

We wanted what only they were selling, part of which was their eccentricity.

These leaders had, and still have, an elemental need to build something different. They started something unique, found like-minded people to help them, and stuck around long enough to ensure the brand stayed different. We can be fairly certain that these leaders were told in no uncertain terms, by people supposedly more expert than they, that the thing they wanted to do could not be done. They listened, then they went back to work. How eccentric.

As I write this, I am contemplating a truly eccentric, highly differentiating but highly controversial positioning stance for a client. So eccentric that I'm pretty sure I can't sell it from the outside. So eccentric that it would take an equally eccentric leader to hold an authentic worldview for the brand in question. So eccentric that I need another idea.

5. GET TO KNOW SIR ISAAC NEWTON'S LAW OF INERTIA.

Marketers love to look at trends. They love to listen to trend experts, most of whom drive me crazy, as they seem to define trends only as naming opportunities, mere observations. Yes, finding and riding a trend can be good for business, but finding and riding a trend is also an obvious move. Therefore it is not, generally speaking, a strongly differentiated move. Unless you get onto that wave early and stake an ownership claim of some kind. Unless, better yet, you can find a unique position that's informed by that trend.

Though he wasn't talking specifically about trends, Sir Isaac Newton's third law applies here: "For every action there is an equal and opposite reaction." The creative side of my brain is less interested in the "action" part—the trend—and more intrigued by the "equal and opposite reaction" part. For every trend, there will emerge one or more countertrends. If the trend has everyone going low-fat, ride the wave if you can stay on the crest, but know that everyone and their dog will be right there, riding it with you. Instead, take a close look at the opposite reaction: come out with the "fat burger" or the "triple-cheese pizza" or the "super-rich ice cream."

The opposite reaction might not be equal, but there will be far fewer marketers trying to master it. Because it will seem counter-intuitive, it will be more culturally noisy. Those of us looking for difference should apply this law to any trend we see, as it may be ripe with more unique possibilities. If everyone's competing to have the lowest prices, go high-end. If it's all about luxury, go Spartan. If everyone is building gas-guzzling SUVs, build a hybrid. When everyone starts building and buying hybrids, bring back a muscle car. If everyone is pushing digital communication, push intimate, handcrafted communication using high-quality, sensuous paper and pens. And so on.

You can also stretch this law into communication. Almost every category develops a verbal and visual language that permeates its communication. Maybe it's because people are conservative and more comfortable doing what others do. Maybe it's because they're all looking at the same research, or because a strong leader takes one approach and others follow. Whatever the reason, if you create a wall of category print ads, outdoor posters, and online banners, or a video "clutter reel," you'll generally see a certain sameness about the work, a language convention of some kind in play.

Is this the case in your category? Yes? Perfect. Now find a way to do the opposite. Break the convention. Break the rules. Do something different.

There's a VC company named Bedrock Capital, run by a couple of fascinating guys, Geoff Lewis and Eric Stromberg. Both were successful entrepreneurs before getting into the VC business. Their point of view is at once unique and refreshing, and yes, it reflects many of my beliefs about difference, applied directly to the world of venture capital. Bedrock Capital looks for difference in a form they call "narrative violations." This is a pull from their website:

> Our primary shared value is radical open-mindedness; we constantly question popular narratives in search of hidden truths. We believe this is especially useful in venture investing, where capital tends to be dramatically over-allocated to startups that align with the strongest market narratives. Rather than chase the narrative, Bedrock's approach is to invest in promising companies that are underestimated precisely because they are incongruent with the storyline. Our starting point, therefore, is to search for narrative violations. When we find one, we do the work to build passionate conviction in opportunities that most overlook.

How do they do this? The Bedrock partners explain:

> Rather than chase popular narratives, Bedrock's approach is to invest when companies are incongruent with the narrative. Simply put, we search for narrative violations.

> The term narrative violation aptly describes many of today's greatest technology investment opportunities. They are either too one-of-a-kind to fit with the popular narratives of the day, or they violate what the narrative gatekeepers deem plausible or possible.

> Founders Fund invested in SpaceX shortly after their second rocket blew up; the popular narrative

was that the company was about to blow up as well. Andreessen Horowitz's second investment was in Skype, at a time when the popular narrative was that Skype was in a death spiral. When Geoff invested in Lyft in 2012, Uber was still just a black car business. The popular narrative then was that the peer-to-peer model pioneered in large part by Lyft would never work, and even if it did Uber's ruthlessness would crush Lyft. Almost nobody predicted that Uber's ruthlessness would nearly crush Uber.

Believing in an idea that violates the popular narrative is lonely. Building a company around that idea is doubly lonely for entrepreneurs. It entails all the challenges of building something new from scratch, but offers none of the status game advancement bestowed upon entrepreneurs pursuing "popular" opportunities. They don't slot easily into technology trend pieces or analyst reports on hot categories. They aren't buzzed about by venture capitalists at the myriad of startup networking events around the world. As a result, these companies are granted immunity from clone wars by narrative shade that can last for years. They also remain systematically underestimated by investors. By the time the popular narrative catches up to begin resembling truth, these companies have grown beyond their fragile early days. And at that point—when they have bent the narrative toward a new reality by sheer force of will—they have already become unstoppable.

They sign off with a killer finish: "The best time to invest in a company is when it's most in violation of a popular narrative."

These guys are very successful VCs, not marketing strategists. Or are they successful VCs because they're marketing strategists? Either way, Bedrock understands the power of difference. They are, quite literally, betting on it.

To wrap up this point, and because I can, let me quote Clint Eastwood: "There's a rebel lying deep in my soul. Anytime anybody tells me the trend is such and such, I go the opposite direction. I hate the idea of trends. I hate imitation; I have a reverence for individuality."

6. THERE'S NO SUCH THING AS A COMMODITY, JUST COMMODITIZED THINKING.

According to Boston Consulting Group, commoditization occurs when the market perceives products to be substitutable. Other definitions go as far as to characterize competing products as indistinguishable in a commodity setting. When difference is nonexistent, variables such as price and distribution obviously play a more prominent role, and margins generally decline accordingly.

On hearing my perspective on the c-word, a friend of mine said he had given a presentation by starting with a slide that broke the word into two parts—*commode* and *oddity*, as a telegraphic abbreviation for the idea that you are tossing your difference down the toilet.

For anyone who talks about their product or service as a commodity, I have a strong and heartfelt suggestion: assume there is no such thing as a commodity category, only commoditized thinking. Or, as Philip Kotler said, "There is no such thing as a commodity. It is simply a product waiting to be differentiated." Yes, at times categories assume commodity characteristics, but this is just a long-term failure of the imagination. Generally, whenever a category does start to look commodity-like, someone comes along with an unexpected, highly differentiated product, service, or position and kicks some category ass.

So-called commodity categories are just categories waiting for someone to create difference.

If Apple didn't exist, most people would see PCs as a commodity category. To be fair, I think most marketers do approach this market as a commodity, but Apple certainly does not. I'm sure vacuum cleaners looked like a commodity until Dyson came along, and now we have a couple of robots creating category noise. Printers have been commoditized for a while now, so who's going to disrupt that picture?

Water is, by definition, a commodity, but don't tell that to brands that have successfully created difference—from Perrier and evian to Fiji and Smartwater. Today that difference has left the building, as people returned to their faucets to source water (such a revolutionary idea), so who will step forward to de-commoditize water once more, and how will they do so? And wasn't coffee pretty commodity-like until Starbucks, Nespresso, and Keurig came along?

When any category is characterized by lots of small, effectively meaningless differences, it has handed its customer a map without any landmarks. All those small differences, no matter what they might mean to their owners, blend into one homogeneous category map for the customer. This sea of sameness unfairly places the navigational onus completely on the customer. Leaving your customer without a guide is not a winning strategy.

Commodity categories call for noncommoditized thinking. They are a silent plea for difference.

7. YOU ARE THE EXPERT IN THE ROOM.

I have a love-hate relationship with customer research. I love it as input, but only as long as we all agree to follow a golden rule:

Customers and consumers are not the marketing experts; we are. I find it a bit amusing to watch a focus group discussion that features six to eight people who are willing to be paid a hundred dollars for two hours of their time on one side of the glass, and six to eight experienced, highly paid marketers on the other side, hanging on to every word. Surely two hours of intensive discussion and debate between those same marketers would yield a better outcome? But hey, often I'm one of those marketers, and I know sometimes the "answer" does originate in those focus groups—perhaps not as something a person on the other side of the glass has said, but as a thought triggered in my mind by the discussion.

A quick sidebar: Despite the fact that I still use it occasionally, consider banning the word *consumer* from your organization. To me, this word connotes a mindless horde of people who exhibit some form of group behavior, a swarm that can be directed en masse. I find this idea a bit insulting and, more importantly, strategically misleading. Much better to consider your *customers*, which, to me at least, connotes people of value who think as individuals. End of sidebar. Back to customer research.

Your audience can tell you what they want, and they can give you valuable input, but they cannot be expected or allowed to make your decisions for you.

In some ways, your audience are difference-killers because they will generally ask for what they don't have. In the book *Different*, Youngme Moon made this point by comparing Volvo and Audi. Audi customers already had style and performance, while Volvo customers already had safety. If you asked them what more they wanted, the Volvo customer would ask for more style and performance, while the Audi customer would ask for more safety. In a universe absent of opportunity cost, you can give everyone everything they want. But in the real world, attempting to give everyone everything comes with a huge opportunity cost. I could say a lot more about that, but for my immediate purposes, let's focus on this problem:

the desire to give everyone everything creates loss of focus, weakens positioning, and confuses the resulting marketing effort. In this case, Volvo got more stylish and their marketing started to talk about performance. In other words, they strayed from their differentiated advantage and, in doing so, placed their brand in jeopardy. As it turned out, they created an opening that Subaru was only too happy to walk through.

As I have said, difference is a lesson in sacrifice. True difference has a price. To be great at one thing, you need to be prepared to give up other things. Easy to understand conceptually, but tough advice to follow in real life.

When researching food, people will inevitably tell you that the most important thing is taste, which might lead an inexperienced marketer to position their product as "great tasting" in some way. Well, great taste is only differentiating in a world where everyone else is claiming bad taste, so you've got to get past this to find something truly unique to say.

In the world of packaging design, a specific research bias is generally well understood. By and large, shoppers will opt for a current design over a new one. This bias toward the known is basic human psychology at work. That can't be ignored. But sometimes a marketer knows that change must happen. They must take this expected customer reaction with a grain of salt and some good professional judgment.

While I'm on this subject, to a marketer who is considering a name or design change, I always make a simple suggestion: don't make any decision up front. In other words, when you decide you are definitely changing your name or design, you are then subject to choosing the best new name or design you can come up with. The risk is that you pick the best of a bad or mediocre bunch, because you're committed to a change and a specific timing for that change. Instead, go through the creative exercise to develop the best possible design or the best possible name. Then do the research, pit the best alternative against what you have, and only then decide if making the change is justified.

One last illustration on the subject of research. Pre-COVID, I was watching an apparel-retailing phenomenon called Brandy Melville. In a ridiculously crowded apparel marketplace, Brandy Melville differentiates itself by offering only one size and, seemingly as a consequence, low prices. If you asked girls (their target audience) if they'd shop a retailer that sells only one size, you would get a hard no. But that is an intellectual response to a rational question. It completely ignores the emotional dynamics of young girls and their clothing. The Brandy Melville craze may or may not have staying power, but pre-COVID, at least, their stores were absolutely packed.

8. SUBTRACTION IS OFTEN BETTER THAN ADDITION.

Businesses have a somewhat automatic response to competition: addition. When faced with competitive parity of some kind, the path to better is seen as purely additive. Likewise, for the undifferentiated, the path to difference is most often seen as a search for something to add.

On the other hand, I think most people would generally agree that, as a culture, we're not craving more, we're craving less. We're craving simplicity. Amid today's clutter and complexity, the most effective path to difference might actually be to take things away.

In one sense, all brands simplify. They act as shorthand for a wealth of information we just aren't willing to take the time to dig into. Apple is a great case in point, as they hide a ridiculously complex technology behind a ridiculously simple, elegant human interface. For obvious reasons, most of us will pay more for simplicity than for complexity. Simplicity sells.

Uber simplifies. Alexa simplifies, as does its parent company, Amazon. Google simplifies.

When you look at success through subtraction, there's an interesting set of examples to discuss.

- Southwest subtracted seat choice and frilly extras and gave us a more democratic, faster boarding process applied with joy.
- IKEA took away pushy salespeople, stuffy stores, and a long-term commitment to our furniture and gave us lightness, fun, and low prices.
- Walmart took away price promotions and gave us the reliability of everyday low pricing.
- Whole Foods took away products that didn't meet their all-natural standards and gave us food we could trust.
- Brandy Melville took away size choice.

If you're looking at a category with an eye toward innovation (your own or something adjacent), try both addition and subtraction. Addition will be automatic, easy to imagine. But can you create a meaningful, differentiated advantage by removing something for the customer? Give it a try and see what you come up with.

9. DIFFERENCE DRIVES INNOVATION.

Yes, I have a hammer, so everything looks like a nail, but I also happen to believe that differentiated advantage makes innovation much easier and much more powerful.

According to Nielsen, 85 percent of all new products fail. Why?

There are a few glaring problems with the "innovation industry." First, it operates on the assumption that innovation can be applied from the outside, which I find to be a strange notion. Companies need to innovate, yes. But if they have to bring consultants in to do so, there's probably something organizational and/or cultural that needs to be addressed before innovations can take root.

The second and larger problem is the way innovation is measured—by number of ideas rather than by real-world results. This "More is better" mindset is completely counterproductive. When it comes to innovation, less is more. A few highly differentiated, strategically powerful ideas, executed perfectly and with sufficient marketing mass to change behaviors, will have a bigger impact than dozens of scattershot ideas. Look for ideas that have true power. Unique ideas that can stand the test of competitive challenge because of their inherent strategic strength.

Third, innovative products must be paired with disruptive, difference-based marketing strategy and execution. Too often this doesn't happen. In fact, when we work with clients in "innovation," we always ask, "What failures have occurred in the past that you felt should have succeeded?" Inevitably the group's answers lead to a single common-sense conclusion: many great ideas have failed through poor execution. Separating the strength of an idea from its strength of execution can be incredibly enlightening, and this simple question often yields some really great ideas.

I watched this happen with Levi's. They had developed a set of products for young men, with a range of really cool features, from the strength of Kevlar to water, odor, and stain resistance. Young guys loved these products. These were jeans they could "go to battle" in. Someone could spill beer on them, but no one would ever know! Imagine the marketing possibilities. With a great positioning strategy behind them, I knew these jeans would be a hit. But that didn't happen. Later, when walking through a store with the Levi's president, I mentioned how much I had loved this idea, and how disappointed I was that it was never launched. He walked over to a display, dug through a bunch of jeans, and found one of those products, declaring, "Yes, they were launched, but they didn't do very well." A real "launch" would have disruptively positioned these jeans to their audience, but we'll never know what a proper consumer launch could have accomplished. As far as the real world is concerned, this product innovation never actually happened.

Fourth, in parallel with strategic product innovation, brands should also engage in a constant, ongoing quality-improvement effort through smaller-scale innovation. It won't change the world, but it's essential. Once again, Apple is the master of this sort of incremental innovation. A commitment to ongoing improvement recognizes that the world is an escalator constantly moving down. If you are standing still, you are losing ground.

In other words, I believe in strategic innovation. Innovation that is driven and inspired by differentiated advantage, made easier by the presence of difference and made more powerful by the "Less is more" maxim. Too many new products are wishful. If your intended audience is anything less than highly enthusiastic, move on to the next idea.

Allow me to enlist the aid of Mark Zuckerberg, who may carry slightly more credibility than I. He said: "There are different ways to do innovation. You can plant a lot of seeds, not be committed to any particular one of them, but just see what grows. And this really isn't how we've approached this. We go mission-first, then focus on the pieces we need and go deep on them and be committed to them." Strategic innovation.

A few years ago, we did a very large innovation project for a brand that will remain nameless. Our research team conducted focus groups as the client team and I looked on from behind the glass. We had created an incredibly long, often silly list of possible innovations, and one by one we were presenting them to the target audience. Could this brand do this? Could this brand do that? Idea after idea met the same answer: sure they could. The client team became more excited with each affirmative response we received, so I sent in a note asking our moderator to pose a different sort of question: Why? Why did people think this brand could do anything? We got the answer I expected: the brand didn't really stand for anything, so within very broad reason, it could do anything it wanted. When we pushed hard, asking if they would really buy a specific innovation from the brand, the answer was "probably not." In the real world, "probably not" is a definite no.

This was a brand without a clear, differentiated positioning strategy. It needed to take a step back and build a positioning strategy based on differentiated advantage. Once it had its positioning strategy squared away, that strategy could inform a couple of big, bold product innovations that could both drive the business and cement the brand position.

New products and brand extensions must have power. Customer permission simply tells you that you can do something, not that you should do it. You need permission plus the power of differentiated advantage. That's difference-based innovation.

10. THINK BEFORE YOU BLINK.

As we go about this process of creating differentiated advantage, we need to be comfortable with the idea that difference is created, not constructed. We need to use both sides of our brain, building the opportunity through analysis and realizing it through some form of intuitive leap.

Your goal: know everything. Strive to be more analytically rigorous than your competitors, but also assume that they're looking at the same data and probably arriving at very similar conclusions. As we heard in the movie *The Incredibles*: "When everyone is super, no one is."

Build that veritable mountain of information, but then climb up, look around, and decide which way to leap. Use the science to get you to the top, then use the art to guide that leap. Information is ubiquitous. Analysis is a given. True brand differentiation and sustainable advantage can be created only in one place—your imagination.

This all sounds good, but most marketers operate within large organizations, and most large organizations aren't exactly known for following the intuitive leaps of their marketers. So once you've made that leap, you will probably also need to put that analytical hat back on to connect that mountain of information to wherever your leap took you. You're going to have to sell your leap to everyone else. Do so knowing that no amount of analysis can substitute for the right intuitive leap.

The irony of this situation can be quite irritating at times, so be prepared. To justify a difference-based position, you will almost certainly be asked to compare your intended path to the paths taken by others. You've chosen a road forward that's never been driven, and those around you will want to know why you can't just take the freeway. The freeway is smooth and straight, and you can drive it so much faster, if only all those other cars would just get out of the way!

In *Blink*, Malcolm Gladwell presented the thesis that we make an intuitive, gut-level decision about events and people in a few seconds (at most). He argued we should go with our gut more, and he provided lots of interesting rationale for why we should, as well as tips for training that gut. While I wholeheartedly agree with his central thesis, I disagree with the way he stretches it to the point of encouraging us all to just go ahead and make whatever decision "feels" right.

At the other end of the spectrum, "Better Branding," from the *McKinsey Quarterly* (2003, no. 4), suggests that "marketers rely too much on intuition." McKinsey is a great company filled with smart, highly analytical thinkers, but they really don't have a clue about building differentiated brands. They are brand "managers," not builders, and their style would result in a long-term (but extremely well-managed) decline.

Gladwell and McKinsey both make valid points, but these points are incomplete and open to misinterpretation when it comes to real-world marketing and brand building. To abuse the titles of two very different business books: you've got to Think, then you've got to Blink.

Great brands are built through differentiation. Great tactics are differentiated, and therefore they cut through the clutter of marketing and everyday life. If you want to be different—truly different—an intuitive leap must surely occur at some part of the process. No amount of analytical rigor will get you to a truly differentiated idea. If you can "think" your way there, assume everyone else has already been there before you. As Andy Grove (of Intel fame) said when quoting his favorite professor, "When everybody knows that something is so, it means that nobody knows nothin'."

If you follow all of this advice, what have you done? You've conducted a thorough investigation, leaving no stone unturned. Knowing that others also have done this, you've used this analysis as grist for the creative mill. You've used it as a springboard from which you have taken several alternative intuitive leaps. Then you've asked the customer to help you select and refine the optimal direction.

Anyone can do the analysis. (Assume everyone will do the analysis.) Anyone can create intuitive leaps out of thin air. It's only when you do both that the magic happens.

Knowledge → Organization → Creativity → Proof

This is what makes it so tough to be a great marketer. You've got to be sufficiently analytical to organize and build that mountain of research, *and* you've got to be creative and courageous enough to leap off that mountain in the direction your intuition tells you to. Left brain, meet right brain.

"Each one of you has something no one else has, or has ever had: your fingerprints, your brain, your heart. Be an individual. Be unique. Stand out. Make noise. Make someone notice. That's the power of individuals."

—Jon Bon Jovi

CHAPTER 10

GETTING PEOPLE ON BOARD

*"It has bothered me all my life that I do
not paint like everybody else."*

—Henri Matisse

Okay, you get it now. You understand the power of difference. You're itching to flex your DQ and launch your brand to icon-level greatness. But how do you get everyone else on board with you? Here it is: an entirely practical guide to gaining organizational support for finding differentiated advantage, then exercising that difference in the most impactful way possible. There is no particular order or ranking of importance to the eight ideas presented here; just read through them now, and perhaps come back to them when you find yourself in internal selling mode.

I know some of these suggestions can be extremely hard to follow within the real life of an organization, but no one said this would be easy. Doing different is hard. Getting other people to do different along with you can be harder.

1. PREPARE YOUR ORGANIZATION
FOR WHAT IS TO COME.

To get your organization on board with difference, you need to lift their sights. Sell the endless possibility of a truly differentiated marketplace position. A truly differentiated position tells you what to do, thereby making everyone's job so much easier. Placing your business or brand on a growth trajectory will yield benefits for many years to come. In the long term, difference can be the catalyst that vaults your business from mediocrity to success.

Once you get your organization digging into difference, remember that for every differentiated position, there is a hard version and a soft version. You must find a way to sell and stick with the hard version. It will seem more extreme. Eccentric. A bit too absolute. But stick with it, because the soft version is an early sign of compromise, of fuzziness creeping in to make the idea more palatable for the low-DQ members of your organization. To really make this work, you need to find a way to do the hard version.

2. USE ANALOGS TO INSPIRE AND
MOTIVATE THE SKEPTICS.

People less brave than you will ask you to prove the track record of your idea, but if your idea is sufficiently different, by definition it won't have a track record. Use analogs instead. This book is full of examples of difference-based strategies, with more examples of difference-based communication campaigns still to come. Argue for the massive rewards inherent to "blue oceans" and moving from "zero to one." Again, consider the gap between Dove as a bar of soap before "Real Beauty" and Dove as a line of beauty products— that's growth based solely on a highly differentiated and immensely compelling brand point of view. We are talking about $4.5 billion annually, and who couldn't use an additional $4.5 billion in their pocket, every . . . single . . . year?

3. ENSURE YOU'VE BUILT A NOISY STRATEGY.

When I say noisy strategy, I mean a strategy that will, almost naturally, lead to disruptive, culturally impactful tactics the audience will pay attention to, talk about, share. This strategy doesn't just place your brand in the right position; it inspires the people who will use it, such that they start seeing noisy tactical interpretations of your strategy the minute you pitch it.

In fact, sometimes the best way to sell a strategy is through tactical examples. Move from "We think this" to "We do this." When we were selling a positioning strategy to Xbox years ago, we mocked up a bunch of fun tactical interpretations of the strategy, to show how it might come to life. The position was based on the fact that, at that point in time, Xbox Live was significantly superior to the Sony online gaming alternative. On Xbox Live you could easily game with friends, which is really the heart of gaming. I recall a T-shirt that read: "If you want to play with friends, use Xbox. If you want to play with yourself, use PlayStation." Our point was, if a bunch of strategy types can do this, imagine what a truly creative communication partner could do with the position.

Not only can this help you sell the idea, but it also gives you the opportunity to pressure-test its potential to create that cultural noise. It shows that partners are behind your idea. It enlists support internally and across your agency partners.

4. WAIT FOR SOMETHING GREAT.

I've mentioned this one before, and I think it's important enough to mention again. Too many marketers build a plan, then start creative communication development. Because they've committed to a plan, and perhaps even purchased media, they launch their new position with what is essentially the best content their agencies could create in the time allotted. They go with the best available rather than insisting on something truly noisy. Do not let this happen in your organization. You're looking for the integration of significant business opportunity, differentiated positioning, and excellence in content creation, and you shouldn't loosen the purse strings until you're confident of all three.

Look at some of the examples listed in chapter 11. Insist on something of this caliber. Do not settle. You owe your company something disruptive and compelling, so do whatever you have to do to create it. Run an agency review so you can increase the odds. Find the best creative team in the world, buy them a drink, and offer them a million dollars. I don't care—just get something truly great before you commit to a launch plan. You'll be amazed at how much easier it is to get the go-ahead, and a significant support budget, when you have a brilliant campaign in your hand. Assume you have only one chance to leap through that open window, so you've got to leap as far as possible.

5. LAUNCH THE POSITION INTERNALLY.

Particularly if you're in a service business of any kind, launch your position internally before you do so externally. It's strange to me that people will buy media based on the premise that it takes three or more impressions to make an attitudinal dent in their audience, but they will launch their new strategy internally through a single company-wide meeting. Before you launch externally, take the time and care to consistently guide and inspire your people, so they can consistently guide and inspire your customer. Building internal support for difference, across your company, will pay long-term dividends, for you and your business.

In service (and we're all in service), never forget that brands are built from the inside out. No amount of paid communication spending will overcome a customer experience that is inconsistent with the promise being made. Consider cautionary tales like that of Sears, which once launched a great apparel campaign titled "The Softer Side of Sears" despite knowing that they had the featured apparel in only some of their stores and had just let many of their salespeople go. When United Airlines ran a campaign called "Rising," their flight attendants were both angered and embarrassed by their inability to create the kind of service that might have lived up to this claim. United's people were trying hard, but quite rightfully they felt they were dropping, not rising.

6. BUILD CRITICAL MARKETING MASS.

Remember the Coke machine metaphor? To do difference well, you've got to argue against spreading marketing dollars too thin. If your organization can't afford a massive national campaign, don't settle for a minor one or you and your strategy are destined to fail. Instead, restrict the geography and do it right. If you can't afford to reach the target audience effectively, find a way to further prioritize and screen that audience. Marketers conduct "test markets," but consider a "How high is up?" market, where you restrict scale but optimize all the dimensions of your marketing effort. Learn, in a real-world situation, the upside potential of your product or service. It's amazing how many companies and marketers go through life never knowing the true upside for their products and services. Don't let your company make that mistake.

Once you have those incredible results gained in a limited market, sell your organization on the larger opportunity.

7. WAR-GAME YOUR STRATEGY.

Prepare your organization to war-game the hell out of your positioning strategy. Brands compete against other brands, but also against ideas. Which brands and ideas might create obstacles to success? Which brands and ideas might represent a more mutually beneficial partnership? Don't simply analyze these brands and ideas; assume their position and actively seek to destroy your proposed position. What might they do, and how will you bake these possibilities into your planning?

This approach shows others you've fully thought through your strategy. Better, it will inevitably cause you to refine, even significantly modify, your plan. This is going to take some coaxing and leadership on your part, but it's worth it.

At Kellogg's, every year we would break the marketing, sales, finance, and advertising agency teams into three. We assigned each team a key competitor, and they set about analyzing possible actions the competitor might take, then planning our responses to those actions. In other words, we wrote our competitors' marketing plans before we wrote ours. One year, a competitor played out every single action we predicted, and we were ready for all of them. Our success that year led directly to the competitor exiting the market. (I later discovered that one of our agency people had applied for a job with the competitor's agency and had been taken on a tour through their plan. In hindsight, I'm not sure this was legal, but it certainly was effective.)

8. MEASURE DIFFERENCE.

It's an old saw for a reason: If it gets measured it does get done. When you only measure standard financial and competitive dimensions (such as shipments and market share), there's a very real risk that their measurement and subsequent pursuit will lead to incrementalism. When you measure difference, your organization has a much more accurate picture of where your brand sits in the minds of your audience. When you measure difference, there's a greater chance that your organization will embrace bigger, more imaginative leaps in brand positioning and product innovation. Difference is a leading indicator, therefore measuring it can give you a sense of what's coming and an opportunity to prepare for it. In short, if you can get your organization to measure difference, you're more likely to get them to do different.

If you are a high-DQ marketer in a low-DQ organization, steering your people toward difference will not be easy, but it will be worth it. While I'd love to think that all good businesspeople will respect a truly powerful differentiated strategy, I've been in too many meetings where people failed to do so. As a consultant, I believe we owe our clients the absolute best advice, as well argued as possible. Anything else is a cheat. But I'd be lying if I said it wasn't frustrating—even demoralizing at times—when great advice goes unused. At the end of the day, though, the juice is very much worth the squeeze.

"Don't you ever let a soul in the world tell you that you can't be exactly who you are."
—Lady Gaga

CHAPTER 11

DIFFERENCE IN EXECUTION

"The problem isn't that we aim too high and fail,
it's that we aim too low and succeed."
—Sir Ken Robinson

I have now worked in the area of marketing strategy for more years than I like to count, and there's one sentence I continue to utter every time we get to the business of finalizing a positioning strategy of any kind: It's only a great strategy if it makes for great execution.

For any circumstance we may find ourselves in, there is a range of intellectually correct positioning strategies and a much wider range of ways in which we might articulate those strategies. Ideas matter most, so the key is finding the correct positioning strategy, but the words you use to articulate it will also count, particularly when it's time to execute.

In other words, the position, whatever it is, must guide and inspire disruptive execution. An intellectually correct strategy that doesn't inspire disruptive execution is simply not as valuable as one that does. It's not wrong, but it's not right enough. This is why it's so important that our positioning strategies are as difference based as possible.

I've been a working marketer and I have worked in advertising, so I can fall back on that experience as we pull a positioning strategy together. The communication campaigns I imagine are totally lame in comparison to the work of a great agency partner, but if I'm not seeing the executional potential of the idea, I know we still have work to do on our strategy.

It's only a great strategy if it makes for great execution.

To push this line of thought even further, great strategy drives great tactics, but the reverse can also be true. Great tactics should influence, and can sometimes even drive, great strategy. Of course, as a strategy consultant, I'll argue that strategy is most important, but this is primarily because it sets the direction. It's the point of origin. Without it you're like the old comic strip character, Pogo: "Having lost sight of our objective, we redoubled our effort." Put differentiated strategy first and then add disruptive tactics, and you've got a $1 + 1 = 3$ equation.

Let's take a closer look at this highly synergistic relationship between strategy and tactics.

Attention is the currency of marketing. Or, as Kevin Kelly said more eloquently in *Wired*, "The only factor becoming scarce in a world of abundance is human attention." Yesterday's marketing model could assume attention, therefore it could focus on "out-persuading" the competition. Today's marketing model simply cannot assume attention. For today's marketer, attention is—and for the foreseeable future will be—an increasingly hard-earned and critical currency.

Find a way to gain attention and then, once you've earned it, consider a more subtle, honest, and interactive form of persuasion. Today's audience is more marketing savvy than ever before. Your product or service is not perfect, so don't pretend it is. Talk to your audience the way you would talk to a friend in conversation, not the way you would address a crowd of strangers with a megaphone.

This is where difference in execution can indeed be as important as difference in strategy.

To get attention, find the executional pattern and break with it. If people talk fast and loud, speak slow and soft. If people use color, go black and white. When almost every marketer approaches their brand with rose-colored glasses, telling us how perfectly amazing it is, consider telling the unvarnished truth. Consider "reality-based marketing." Strangely enough, an authentic sense of reality remains a fairly revolutionary idea in most marketing circles.

Someone once compared the BMW brand site to a site run by enthusiastic BMW owners and fans. The brand website is award winning, polished, and elegant. To BMW's credit, it's state-of-the-art in many ways. In this environment, the car is perfect. Beautiful. Flawless. Conversely, on the fan site, owners talk about their cars and the BMW brand with deep affection, but also with honesty. The fan site is authentic. It feels real. The brand site is propaganda, and therefore it's taken with a grain of salt, even by those very same fans. Stop and consider: Do you really believe your brand is perfect? Do you really think your customers find it perfect? Do you think they find anything in their lives perfect? Why not make noise with the truth in all that?

In 2019, after revamping everything about their somewhat troubled brand, Carlsberg ran a campaign with the headline "Probably Not the Best Beer in the World," a riff on their historic "Probably the Best Beer in the World" campaign. While an incredibly brave and provocative move, this was a brand that was destined to ride off into the sunset if something disruptive wasn't done. They were ready for a last-ditch effort. Brand bravery is easy to talk about, but much harder to do, even when it's your only chance at survival. It's too early to tell if this worked for Carlsberg, but brand awareness immediately shot up.

I worked with Red Bull for years. Rumors abounded about that product. Early on, people actually believed the drink included bull testicles as an active ingredient. At another point, a false story was circulating that five Scandinavian teens had died from a Red Bull overdose. As an experienced marketer, I asked the obvious question: "How do we derail these rumors and get the truth out?" The head of marketing looked at me with a knowing, almost pitying smile and said, "We do nothing at all." A few seconds went by, then things clicked into place. Red Bull knew exactly what it was: a global bad boy. It was far from a perfect citizen, not to mention the product didn't even taste all that good to many people. But Red Bull was real, and people responded to it that way.

In early 2020, Burger King removed all artificial colors, flavors, and preservatives from their Whopper. To drive this product improvement home, they created an ad showing a thirty-four-day time-lapse video of a fresh-from-the grill Whopper decaying into an ugly, moldy burger, set to the tune "What a Difference a Day Makes," and followed by the line "The beauty of no artificial preservatives." As one viewer commented, "Someone's either going to get fired or promoted over this." That someone is their highly talented CMO, Fernando Machado, who very obviously embraces the need to do something different if you actually want to grab attention. Some viewers laughed and some moaned, but they all noticed and remembered. A very clever idea from Burger King's agency, yes, but also a very, very brave move by their CMO.

Human beings are imperfect, and we tend to feel more at ease with, more connected to, people who acknowledge their own imperfections. Intellectually we know our brands are also imperfect, but brands have never been comfortable admitting it. Once upon a time, we learned to accept this dishonesty. We expected marketers to tell white lies. Put more bluntly, to be bullshit artists. But, let's face it, in today's world the truth will win out sooner, not later. If we don't assume total transparency, we risk our customers' trust and loyalty. We might as well bring this transparency to our marketing tactics. What if we stop trying too hard to look perfect? What if we take off those rose-colored glasses? Instead of fearing your imperfections, maybe you should celebrate them. Yes, I understand this is a step too far for most companies, but just consider how you might breathe more authenticity and realism into the way you go to market.

To stretch the point even further, instead of seeming like a brand in constant pursuit of more people, maybe take a risk and play a bit hard to get. Like the "Soup Nazi" from *Seinfeld*. An owner of a small shop, the Soup Nazi makes amazing soup, but frequently turns people away because he doesn't like their attitude. Supposedly modeled after a real person, the character is deliberately extreme. But consider brands like Google in its early days. Everyone else was clamoring for our attention, trying to be as "sticky" a "portal" as possible, because that was what supposedly worked best financially. Not Google. You had to discover them, and when you did, all you got was a stripped-down unassuming search box. In using that box, you were in the know. You were smart enough to see through all that marketing fluff to get to the most efficient search experience possible, as defined by Google.

The lesson? Don't pursue so hard. Increase the subtlety. See what happens.

Also, don't borrow interest. This is a pet peeve of mine: marketers spend good money to communicate ideas that people already grasp and readily agree with, then they find some clumsy way to attach their product. This is a lazy person's approach to undifferentiated communication. Don't be lazy. Assume that every product or service has an inherent, unique drama, and you just need to find it. Until you do, hold on to your money.

Remember your goal: break patterns to get noticed by real people with busy lives.

Consider this: Over the past ten to fifteen years, the number of brands on US supermarket shelves has tripled, and the number of advertising messages we're exposed to has more than doubled. We've gone from a few television channels to thousands of program options. Information is ubiquitous. The average American adult now spends eleven and a half hours a day on a screen of some kind, and everything on those screens is vying for their attention. In this world, there is no time or space for gray. In this world, you have to behave differently if you want anyone to pay attention to you.

Despite all of this, ninety-nine percent of marketing communications remain predictable and undifferentiated, and therefore invisible. When I ran a marketing department, I used my "Can't like it" rule for assessing creative work from our agency. Our team could love the agency's work, in which case we would proceed. They could hate it, in which case it was dropped without debate. But we absolutely would not move forward with something we "liked." Like is the enemy of greatness. When you like things, especially as a marketer, you try to improve them. You edit until you like it more, all along becoming more committed to it. You might even make it better, but you absolutely will not make it great. In marketing, "like" is a sucker's game. If you don't truly love it, if you don't find it unique and surprising, do you really believe your audience will pay any attention to it?

The advertising business fascinates me in the same way the entertainment business does. Across the world, large groups of smart, experienced, creative people are gathering together in conference rooms and somehow approving . . . crap. Worse, it's undifferentiated crap. They're approving something with no chance of success, however measured. Somehow, these people convince themselves that this ad, TV show, or movie is going to be great. Do they really believe in its greatness, or do they fall under a spell of some kind? Did they approve it because they thought it was the smart political move? Was it just okay, and they convinced themselves they could make it great? Is this conformity in action? Clearly I've been in those rooms, and I'm also guilty of approving mediocre content, though I'd like to think I've become smarter and more demanding over time.

In general, this behavior is some form of compromise. People tend to go into these meetings with the mindset that they'll run with the best idea that shows up in the room—an expensive mistake. Rather than "This is the best we have, so let's do it," try "I'll hang on to my money until someone shows me something truly great."

To illustrate and inspire, here's a list of truly great brand communication. If you are a working marketer responsible for building a brand, there is absolutely no reason you couldn't be on this list. In fact, you owe it to your brand to get on this list. These are campaigns that made a huge, trajectory-shifting impact on the brands that created them. Some may seem dated now, but time has allowed them to prove their monetary value, which might be measured in the billions. Take a look at the list, then look up the campaigns for fun and inspiration.

- I've talked about Dove and Corona, both examples of highly differentiated and counterintuitive ideas expressed brilliantly through marketing communications.
- Nike has too many amazing campaigns from Wieden+Kennedy to count.
- UNICEF Tap Project—a truly great idea is always the best place to start.
- Absolut—their bottle campaign made this the world's number one vodka.
- Miller Lite—"Tastes Great, Less Filling." Yes, they later lost the script, but what a brilliant piece of positioning that was.
- Always—"Like a Girl." Such a brilliant idea you can't believe they were the first to have it.

- VW—"Think Small." How dare they take a liability and own it? Did they just call their own car a lemon? Check out an ad called "The Force."
- Dos Equis—"The Most Interesting Man in the World." Did he just say, "I don't drink beer"?
- "Got Milk?"—From the glory days of Goodby Silverstein, influenced by one of the agency world's smartest planners.
- Apple—"1984" was arguably the best ad of all time, but their Mac versus PC campaign surely did much more for their business.
- Old Spice—"The Man Your Man Could Smell Like." Who would've guessed you could restage this brand that successfully?
- Wendy's—"Where's the Beef?" Unexpected, fun, and highly competitive.
- Google—"Year in Search." Maybe it shouldn't be on this list, but watch it anyway.
- Burger King—This marketing team has their brand totally dialed in at the moment, and perhaps this is the talented CMO who finally, once and for all, drives home their core differentiated advantage versus McDonald's: the flame.
- I also urge you to look up these recent campaigns, even though it's too soon to test their results. Check out a video titled "Designed by Apple in California." Also find the 2019 Sipsmith Gin campaign, Apple AirPods, Lacoste's "Crocodile Inside," Jif, and the aforementioned Splenda and Halo Top. Brilliance.
- Also, just for kicks, see if you can find the outdoor board for a vibrator from Canada that reads, "Scream your own name!"

Of course, every marketer has their own list of favorites. But at the end of the day, sadly, these lists remain shorter than they should be. In fact, if you made the top 100 marketers and top 100 agency creative directors watch every television ad run in 2019, with the mission of choosing their personal top 50, I bet two things would happen. First, they would fall asleep after the first hundred ads. Second, you would find the same twenty truly amazing ads on every single list. Good marketers know great when they see it.

Now this may seem crazy, but what if a marketer refused to spend any advertising money until they had a campaign of this caliber? Would the advertising business grind to a halt? If you had to wait a couple of extra months to get a campaign of this caliber, would your business grind to a halt? Great campaigns can completely alter the trajectory of a brand and business, year after year after year.

Let me say that again: great campaigns can completely alter the trajectory of a brand and business.

Every brand owner has the ability to create one of these world-changing campaigns, so why don't you? (This is not a rhetorical challenge.) World-changing campaigns are within your grasp. Just remember that they all begin, and end, with difference.

> *"You have your way. I have my way. As for the right way,*
> *the correct way, and the only way, it does not exist."*
> —Friedrich Nietzsche

CHAPTER 12

PARTING THOUGHTS

"We are the ones we've been waiting for.
We are the change that we seek."

—Barack Obama

Before we part, I want to leave you with a request, an appeal, and
a challenge.

A REQUEST

As you can imagine, I value every single word in this book of mine,
but if I had to, could I boil them all down to one simple request? I
think so. Here it is:

Next time you hit a crossroad of any kind, find a piece of paper,
an app, or a whiteboard. Create two columns. In one column, list
the expected solutions, the table stakes, the contextual characteristics of the situation. Now, set this long list aside and ask yourself,
What would an unexpected, totally unique solution look like?

In short, you can't find difference if you aren't looking for it. That's my one request: look for difference. Once you start looking, you've started lifting your DQ.

I lied—turns out I have two requests: look for difference *and* lift your DQ. How? Be yourself. Think for yourself. Find your own difference and embrace it. Work somewhere that truly appreciates the unique contribution only you can make.

AN APPEAL

But what about the DQ of the people around you? How do we raise DQ in organizations?

For better and for worse, I am a working marketer and not any kind of expert on organizational behavior. In my tenure as a CEO, I was too quick to lead with ideas and strategy and too slow to build the organizational structure that could support those strategies. I was too fascinated by the next idea to give focus to what I saw as the less interesting task of organization. Thankfully, not everyone is like me. Many people have a real passion for creating large-scale, purposeful, and therefore successful organizations.

To them, I appeal.

How can we increase the DQ of our people? How do we encourage and reward our people to think and do different? While our people are most certainly the starting point, how can we systematically increase the DQ of our organizations? How do we build organizations that value, create, and nurture difference?

True organizational leaders will structure these questions and their answers in ways I cannot.

I will, however, offer three observations:

First, if you focus on the people, I believe the rest will follow. If and when an organization actively promotes difference, people will step up. Watch and listen to them, as they may come up with solutions and systems you have never considered.

Second, in the many organizations I work with, one litmus test instantly gauges their DQ: their openness to debate. Lack of debate breeds groupthink and bad decision making. Open debate breeds better decision making. Debate breeds difference.

I once had the distinct pleasure of spending a day with Bob Iger and the senior Disney team, brainstorming a design strategy for Disney Stores. Our team is accustomed to pushing clients to think more creatively, and this may have been the only time our team actually had to try to rein in an overly creative client team. Why? Bob Iger was completely open to debate. He actively encouraged it. He would state a position and other team members would tell him he was wrong. He never blinked. He listened attentively, then he either agreed or sought to better support his own perspective. His response was completely natural. Never once did I get the slightest sense of positional power being exercised. I saw the same dynamic occur when an assistant flat-out told Bob he was wrong and I was right. (I liked that assistant.) I had no doubt this group would get to the best solution they were capable of creating, and they would get there as a team. Because ideas would be built on or tossed away based on their merit, regardless of whose ideas they happened to be.

No single person will always make the right decision. Good decisions survive diverse perspectives and intelligent debate. Bad decisions do not.

Leaders who authentically welcome debate will cultivate difference in the organizations they lead. Leaders who discourage debate may find themselves disastrously following their own bad ideas simply because no one dared disagree with them. In this and so many other ways, conformity is bad for business. (It also sucks as a feature of organizational culture.)

A belief in difference encourages debate, and a belief in debate encourages difference.

Third, consider that diversity and difference are highly related ideas. Diverse teams will create better, more holistically considered decisions. Diverse teams will be more innovative. Diverse companies will be more successful. Don't think of diversity as an obligation; view it as an opportunity for competitive advantage.

As I've said, I can answer organizational questions neither artfully nor completely, so I urge real organizational leaders to pick up where I'm leaving off. Because difference—a high-DQ culture—has to start at the top. If leaders do different, they'll get different. Life might feel messier in a high-DQ organization, but it's worth it. Remember, the value between zero and one is exponentially greater than the value between one and two.

A CHALLENGE

Last, but definitely not least, when we talk about difference, there's a larger perspective in play. I challenge you to take a look at it. A close, unflinching look.

When I began writing this book, the concept of DQ was simply an attempt at a catchy, telegraphic way to capture the importance of difference. We have IQ and EQ, surely DQ is just as important? As my exploration of difference progressed, increasingly I leaned into the idea of DQ. Why not create a DQ test? Why not find ways to both measure and promote it—at home, in school, and at work?

Let's blow this up and get dramatic for a moment. This planet of ours is on a road forward, and most of us can see where it ends. We don't know the length of the trip. We don't know its exact details. But surely, we see the destination.

Without doubt, we are actively killing the planet that feeds us. We are creating wealth and health disparities that will most certainly come back to haunt us. In fact, they're haunting too many of us already. Here's a sad fact for you: eight people have as much wealth as half of the human race! Here in the United States, an unacceptably large proportion of our people live without access to health care, without sufficient support systems, and with no viable safety net in sight. Right now, fifty-four million Americans are "food insecure"—worried about their ability to eat tomorrow. This is not *Hunger Games*; this is a civilized society.

Yes, we see the warning signs, we sense the destination, but have we come up with any powerful solutions? No. We willfully look the other way.

As I sit here, finishing this book, I'm waiting for the COVID-19 dust to settle, worrying about future pandemics, climate change, and this gross wealth disparity. Nothing promotes change better than a good old-fashioned crisis. Nevertheless, and with no offense intended, the US presidential election was fought between two white men well into their seventies.

We are running out of time.

How can we change the road we are so clearly on? How can we bring new thinking to old problems? How are we going to create and embrace the kind of groundbreaking, never-before-seen solutions we so desperately need?

Here's an example: We need a high-speed rail connection between San Francisco and Los Angeles. As you would expect, the costs and the conflict around this proposed project rose quickly, and its odds of survival are very low. But along comes this guy named Elon Musk. Expressing his disappointment in the high-speed rail solution, he proposes that a vacuum tube might be a faster, cheaper solution. In May 2013, Musk likened his "Hyperloop" idea to a "cross between a Concorde, a railgun, and an air hockey table."

But wait, it gets better. He open-sourced the idea, and a couple of engineering firms paid attention. They have played with the idea and essentially validated it. They've now built scale models.

It appears this idea may indeed represent a faster, cheaper, much more fuel-efficient alternative to air and road travel. I love this story! Elon Musk is pretty busy running a car company, a solar company, and a space exploration company at the moment, so we need to find others just as smart, just as fearless, and just as different—to identify and implement radical solutions to ongoing problems.

And we need to find them soon.

We need to think different. We need to do different. We need to celebrate and promote DQ in our homes, our schools, our organizations, and ourselves. We need to recognize diversity as a path to DQ. We need to identify difference as a first principle when creating marketing strategy, yes, but also when creating change in the larger systems, customs, and ideologies that govern our lives.

Lest I get too carried away, let me come back to my starting point. First and foremost, I set out to show working marketers how difference drives success. I hope I've convinced you not just to think differently, but to accept nothing less than difference. True, compelling, competitively advantageous difference. You owe this to the idea, person, place, or business you serve. Most importantly, you owe it to yourself.

Thanks for reading.

> *"The best time to plant a tree was twenty years ago. The second best time is now."*
> —Chinese Proverb

"Life should not be a journey to the grave with the intention of arriving safely in a pretty and well-preserved body, but rather to skid in broadside in a cloud of smoke, thoroughly used up, totally worn out, and loudly proclaiming 'Wow! What a Ride!'"
—Hunter S. Thompson

ACKNOWLEDGMENTS

When I wrote the acknowledgments for my first book, I essentially thanked everybody who has helped me along the way. It has taken a village. Hopefully, those of you I thanked actually bought and read the entire book, but I rest assured that you at least read the acknowledgments and know how important your help has been to me.

Once again, I'd like to thank Joe DiNucci and Atiya Dwyer of Silicon Valley Press, without whom neither of my books would ever have made it over the line. For her editing mastery and pandemic writing kinship, I also want to thank Cheryl Dumesnil, who made this book better every time she touched it.

This time, I'd like to thank my longtime colleague, now business partner for the past three years, Alpa Pandya. Her grace, support, and good humor make it fun to walk to my computer to engage with each and every day of the week. And when it comes to marketing strategy, there is simply no one better.

I also want to thank my kids, Andy and Sydney, both now grown up, for the joy they bring to me. An incredibly empathetic teacher and a master of digital media, they could not possibly make their father more proud. And my brother, Saunders, and his wife, Mary Ann, who consistently show me an easier path to a happy life. Also a part of my expanded family over the past several years, my stepdaughter, Annika, is a constant source of joy and pride.

Last but most certainly not least, my muse and wife, JJ. Watching her try to save the world through clean energy makes me feel small. Watching her be my wife and best friend makes me feel very large. Very aware that we only get this one journey, I find that words aren't enough to thank her for taking it with me.

ABOUT THE AUTHOR

Before turning thirty-five, Austin McGhie led a CPG marketing and sales team and a top advertising agency. Since then, he has successfully gotten older, run two more agencies, and built a nationally recognized marketing strategy business from the ground up before selling it to a global communications company. Today, he and his business partner, Alpa Pandya, happily run a small but mighty marketing strategy consulting business, somewhat appropriately named Find Difference. Along the way, Austin has advised clients such as Kellogg's, Disney, Boeing, Nike, ESPN, NBC, YouTube, Levi Strauss, Westin, Amazon, Facebook, Visa, and Unilever.

Austin splits his time between San Francisco and Bodega Bay, with his wife, JJ, and their dog, Chili, surrounded by his beautiful and strongly opinionated nuclear family. In addition to participating in a host of writing and speaking engagements, Austin is the "almost-bestselling" author of *BRAND Is a Four Letter Word: Positioning and the Real Art of Marketing.* Visit him at FindDifference.com.

CPSIA information can be obtained
at www.ICGtesting.com
Printed in the USA
BVHW031417150921
616788BV00007B/27/J